HISTORY

OF

SPRINGFIELD, ILLINOIS,

Its Attractions as a Home and Advantages for Business,

MANUFACTURING, ETC.

PUBLISHED UNDER THE AUSPICES OF THE

SPRINGFIELD BOARD OF TRADE,

BY J. C. POWER.

SPRINGFIELD:
ILLINOIS STATE JOURNAL PRINT.
1871.

CORRESPONDENCE.

SPRINGFIELD, ILL., May. 19, 1871.

MESSRS. S. H. MELVIN, W. B. MILLER and W. B. COWGILL:

GENTLEMEN:—Having placed myself under your direction—as a committee of the Board of Trade—in the preparation of the following pages on the "History of Springfield, Illinois: its attractions as a Home, and advantages for Business, Manufacturing," etc., I hereby submit a copy of the advance sheets for your inspection. It is for you to say whether I have, or have not, redeemed the promises made in my Prospectus of Feb. 27th.

Respectfully, yours, J. C. POWER.

SPRINGFIELD, ILL., May 22, 1871.

J. C. POWER, ESQ.:

DEAR SIR:—We have examined the proof sheets of the "History of Springfield, etc.," as submitted to us on the 19th inst., and cheerfully certify, that, in our judgment, it is all, and *more*, than could have been reasonably expected from your prospectus.

It evinces a great amount of research, and is much more comprehensive than you promised us. We confidently hope and expect that a thorough circulation of your work will materially advance the interests of our beautiful and growing city.

Yours, truly,

S. H. MELVIN,
W. B. MILLER,
W. B. COWGILL,
Committee.

INTRODUCTORY REMARKS.

In laying the result of my labors, for several weeks past, before the people of Springfield, I wish to correct an impression, which prevails to some extent, that this is a directory, or gazetteer, or business mirror of the city. It was not intended for anything of the kind, but just what its title indicates.

The notices of business houses, with but few exceptions, are simply courtesies due to those who assisted me in placing in this form the attractions and advantages of the capital city. It is to these, less than two hundred, business men and firms that the whole 18,000 citizens are under obligations for any good that may accrue to Springfield from this publication. There is a large number of mercantile houses in the city who are not mentioned.

In the business of manufacturing I have endeavored to present the names of all, in order to give every manufacturer living at a distance, an opportunity of knowing whether his particular branch of business is represented or not. A manufacturer, who does not find his business mentioned under the head of "Manufacturing Establishments," may know that this is a clear field.

I must make this an occasion for tendering my thanks to those business men in general, including the Mayor and City Council of Springfield, who have given me their support. To Messrs. Melvin, Miller and Cowgill for their co-operation, advice and assistance. And to the venerable James L. Lamb and Hon. J. S. Bradford, for repeated courtesies. To one and all, individually and collectively, I hereby tender my sincere thanks.

To Mr. Harry C. Watson I am under special obligations, for the articles that bear his name; also for assisting me in collecting and writing up the business notices in these pages. I very much regret being compelled to omit an excellent article written by him, on the State Arsenal. I can only recommend that every visitor to Springfield call on Gen. Dilger, and see for themselves how harmless the implements of war look in time of peace.

It was my intention to present a description of the magnificent, new, fire-proof United States Court and Post Office building. But of course every visitor to Springfield will visit and examine that also. In fact I find that I have scarcely commenced describing the Attractions and Advantages of the Capital City. If its citizens will use what I have written to the best advantage, I entertain some hopes that it will do good. If, however, they do not heartily co-operate in the work, I have already written too much.

Springfield, May 23, 1871.

J. C. P.

TABLE OF CONTENTS.

PRELIMINARY HISTORICAL SKETCH.

The first white men who explored this region of country, were Jesuit Missionaries from New France—now Canada. They visited the southern shores of the great northern lakes, for the purpose of communicating a knowledge of Christianity to the natives.

James Marquette, a Catholic priest, and M. Joliet, a merchant, from Quebec, with two canoes and five men, left Green Bay and went down the Wisconsin river to the Mississippi, entering the latter stream July 17, 1673. They floated down the "father of waters," making frequent stoppages among the Indians, and passed below the mouth of the Ohio. Here they found the savages disposed to be hostile, which caused them to return. On approaching the mouth of the Illinois, on their way up, they were told by the aborigines, that if they would follow the course of that river, their route to the lakes would be much shorter. Taking this advice, the party reached Lake Michigan, at a point near where Chicago now stands. Other Frenchmen came, by the way of Canada and the lakes, and in a few years all this region of country was considered a part of New France. The French being entitled to it by right of discovery, their possession was undisputed for about ninety years.

Difficulties arising between France and England, at home, the British government sent an army of one thousand regular troops, under General Braddock, to make war against the French and their native allies in the new world. General Braddock landed at Alexandria, Virginia, and after increasing his army to twenty-two hundred, by the addition of provincials, he marched to attack Fort Du Quesne, where Pittsburgh now stands. Colonel George Washington, who was well acquainted with the Indian character, accompanied the expedition as a volunteer aid. General Braddock refused to listen to the counsels of Colonel Washington, and the result was the surprise and defeat of his whole army by the French and Indians. The commander was slain in this engagement, which took place July 9, 1755.

In 1758, the English government sent another army, which was more successful. It took fort Du Quesne, and the war raged until 1763, when the fall of Quebec left the English victors; and by the treaty which followed, the whole of New France was ceded to Great Britain.

Previous to the year 1673, this country was known only to the aborigines, or Indians. From the year of its discovery by the explorations of Marquette and Joliet, for more than half a century there was no attempt at organized government. The first effort was made in 1718, when the "Company of the West" was formed in Paris, for the New World. In that year the building of Fort De Chartres was commenced, and when completed was occupied as the military headquarters of the French. It was about sixteen miles above Kaskaskia, in the American bottom, three miles from the bluff, and three-fourths of a mile from the river.

At the time New France was ceded to England, in 1763, Fort De Chartres was occupied by M. St. Ange de Belle Rive, as Commandant and Governor of the Illinois country. He continued in possession of the fort until 1765. In that year Captain Stirling, of the Royal Highlanders, was sent out and took possession of the fort and country, in the name of the British government. This continued to be the headquarters of the British until 1772, when part of the fort was destroyed by a great rise of water in the Mississippi river. The English garrison was then removed to Kaskaskia.

In 1763, the population of what is now the State of Illinois, did not exceed three thousand. About one-third left the country upon its change of masters; so that when the English took possession, the entire population, including French, English and negroes, was about two thousand.

Rev. John M. Peck says: "In olden time, Kaskaskia was to Illinois what Paris is at this day to France. Both were, at their respective days, the great emporiums of fashion, gayety, and I must say, happiness also. In the year 1721 the Jesuits erected a monastery and college in Kaskaskia, and a few years afterwards it was chartered by the French government. Kaskaskia for many years was the largest town west of the Alleghaney mountains. It was a tolerable place before the existence of Pittsburgh, Cincinnati or New Orleans."

THE AMERICAN REVOLUTION.

The English government became fairly settled in their occupation of the country wrested from France, and then commenced that series of Parliamentary enactments, for the taxation of the American Colonies, without allowing them to be represented in her national councils, which led to the revolutionary struggle. Open hostilities commenced at Lexington, Massachusetts, April 19, 1775. Couriers were despatched, on the most fleet-footed horses, and in a very few days the infant colonies were ablaze with excitement, and the call to arms was responded to from Maine to Georgia. The first Congress met at Philadelphia, Sept. 5, 1774, and continued its meetings by successive adjournments, until July 4, 1776, when the American colonies were declared to be free and independent States. The familiar events of the war for independence, followed each other in quick succession, until all parties were engaged in the conflict, along the Atlantic coast; but there were British outposts in the west which had, until 1778, remained undisturbed. It was known that these posts were depots for supplying the Indians with arms and ammunition, that they might practice deeds of cruelty and murder against the frontier settlers. The general government had not power to command, without consent of the States, even the limited resources of the country; but what there was, seemed imperatively demanded on the seaboard. Under these circumstances, Colonel George Rogers Clarke, of Virginia, volunteered to lead an expedition against the British garrisons west of the Alleghanies; and the Governor and Council of Virginia took the responsibility of sending him out. Two sets of instructions were given him. One which was public, was for Col. Clarke to raise seven companies for the protection of Kentucky, and proceed west. The secret and real instructions were for him to raise seven companies, of fifty men each, and proceed to Kaskaskia, and take or destroy the garrison of Fort Gates at that place; and that the object of the expedition must be kept a profound secret. The instructions were given by the Governor at Williamsburgh, then the Capital of Virginia, Jan. 2, 1788. Feb. 4th Col. Clarke left Virginia, for Pittsburgh. He took with him twelve hundred pounds in depreciated currency to defray the expense of the expedition, and raised three companies in Pittsburgh. He procured boats, and with his supplies, arms and ammunition, descended the Ohio river to "Corn Island," opposite the present city of

Louisville, where he was met by Captain Bowman, who had gone down through Kentucky to raise a company of men. When all were assembled on the island he first disclosed to them that his point of destination was Kaskaskia, in the Illinois country. From "Corn Island" Col. Clarke descended with his forces, to Fort Massac, on the west side of the Ohio river, about forty miles above its mouth. The party left their boats at this point, and marched across the country to Kaskaskia, a distance of 120 miles, through an unbroken wilderness. They arrived within sight of the village on the morning of the 4th of July. He concealed the main body of his men, and sent out spies to reconnoitre. At night the men were divided into two bodies, one to take the village and the other Fort Gage. After all was in readiness, with the soldiers drawn up in line on the banks of the Kaskaskia, Col. Clarke delivered a short address to his troops, in which he reminded them that it was the anniversary of the Declaration of Independence, and that they must take the fort and village at all hazards. Fort Gage was a work of considerable strength, mounted with cannon and defended by regular soldiers. So secret had been the movements of the attacking party, and so little were they expected, that they reached the very gates of the fortification unperceived. In addition to this, they were so fortunate as to get into communication with an American belonging to the fort, who led a detachment of soldiers, under the celebrated Simon Kenton, inside, through a back gate. The first intimation the Governor had of their presence, was by Kenton giving him a shake to arouse him from his slumbers. The conquest was achieved without the shedding of a drop of blood.

The mortification of Governor Rocheblave was so great when he found himself a prisoner in the hands of so small a body of raw militia, without having an opportunity to fire a gun, that he refused to acknowledge any of the courtesies extended to him on account of his official position. The only alternative for Colonel Clarke was to send him in irons to the Capital of Virginia.

THE COUNTY OF ILLINOIS.

Soon after the capture of Kaskaskia, Col. Clarke communicated the result of his expedition to the Governor, and expressed his desire to have civil government extended over the conquered territory. An act was passed by the law-making powers of Virginia, in October, 1778, to establish the county of Illinois. "It embraced all that part of Virginia west of the Ohio river, and was probably the largest county in the world, exceeding in its dimensions the whole of Great Britain and Ireland." To speak more definitely, the county of Virginia, called Illinois, embraced the territory now included in the States of Ohio, Indiana, Illinois, Wisconsin and Michigan.

After capturing Fort Gates, the next point to be reduced was Fort St. Vincent, now Vincennes, Indiana. This fortification fell into his hands Feb. 24, 1779, with Governor Hamilton and seventy-nine men. The property captured with this fort was valued at one hundred thousand pounds sterling.

THE FIRST REPUBLICAN OR DEMOCRATIC GOVERNOR OF ILLINOIS.

Until this stage of its history, the Illinois country had been successively under savage, military and monarchical rulers, but now the time for another change was at hand. The first republican Governor of Illinois was no less a personage than the renowned Patrick Henry, the great orator of the American Revolution. He became the Governor of Virginia, in 1776, and continued to hold the office by re-election until 1779. It was in this way that he came to be the first republican or democratic Governor of Illinois.

The law of Virginia establishing the county of Illinois, having been enacted in October, 1778, on the 12th of December following, Governor Henry appointed John Todd civil commandant and Lieutenant Colonel of the new county.

He wrote Commandant Todd a lengthy letter of instructions, in which he says: "The grand objects, which are disclosed to your countrymen, will prove beneficial or otherwise, according to the nature and abilities of those who are called to direct the affairs of that remote country. * * * One great good expected from holding the Illinois, is to overawe the Indians from warring against the settlers on this side of the Ohio." Near the close of his letter, Governor Henry says: "I think it proper for you to send me an express, once in the month, with a general account of affairs with you, and any particulars you may wish to communicate." The headquarters of Commandant Todd, or the seat of government for the county, was at Kaskaskia.

The stay of Colonel Todd, in Illinois, was not of long duration. Being under orders to return to Virginia, he made it convenient to visit his family at Lexington, Kentucky, on the way. While at Lexington, news came that the Indians west of the Ohio, were crossing over into Kentucky. He returned at the head of his command, and was killed at the battle of Blue Licks. Col. Todd was related to the ancestors of Mrs. Lincoln.

In 1780 Congress recommended to the several States having waste, or unappropriated lands, in the western country, to cede it to the United States government for the common benefit of the Union. In January, 1781, Virginia responded to the overture of Congress, by yielding her claims to the territory northwest of the Ohio river, with certain conditions annexed. By an act of Sept. 13, 1783, Congress proposed to comply, in the main, with the wishes of Virginia; but suggested some modification of the terms. On the 20th of December following, the General Assembly of Virginia passed an act accepting the modified terms proposed by the United States Congress. By this settlement the United States was to refund to Virginia all the money that had been expended by that State in her military operations, in conquering and holding the territory. It was also stipulated that a quantity, not exceeding one hundred and fifty thousand acres of land, promised by the State of Virginia, shall be allowed and granted by the United States, to General George Rogers Clarke, and to the officers and soldiers of his regiment, who marched with him, when the forts of Kaskaskia and St. Vincent were reduced, and to the officers and soldiers that were afterwards incorporated into the said regiment. By this act the representatives of that State, in Congress, were instructed and empowered to transfer the territory, by deed, to the United States. The deed was executed March 1, 1784, and signed by Thomas Jefferson, Samuel Hardy, Arthur Lee and James Monroe.

By Virginia protecting the frontier settlers from the cruelties of Indian warfare, she very justly goes down to posterity, with the honor of having donated to the general government, territory from which has grown five of the very best States of the American Union. But while she was generous to the public, she failed to be just to the man who was instrumental in bringing so much honor upon herself. Butler, in his history of Kentucky, speaking of George Rogers Clarke, says: "The government of Virginia failed to settle his accounts. Private suits were brought against him for public supplies, which ultimately swept away his fortune, and with this injustice the spirit of the hero fell, and the General never recovered the energies which had stamped him as one of nature's noble men. At the same time, it is feared that a too extensive conviviality contributed its mischievous effects." The latter was, most likely, the real cause of his misfortunes.

ORDINANCE OF 1787.

July 13, 1787, an ordinance for the government of the Northwestern Territory, was enacted by Congress, and Gen. Arthur St. Clair appeared at Marietta, on the Ohio river, and put the new government in operation. Washington county was the first organized, and included a considerable portion of the State of Ohio. In Feb., 1790, Governor St. Clair and his Secretary, Winthrop Sargent, arrived at Kaskaskia, and organized the county of St. Clair, which embraced more than half the present State of Illinois. The first legislative body for the Northwestern Territory met at what is now Cincinnati, Sept. 16, 1789. On the 3d of October, Gen. Wm. H. Harrison was elected the first delegate to represent the Northwestern Territory in the Congress of the United States.

TERRITORY OF OHIO ORGANIZED.

May 7, 1800, Ohio was provided with a territorial organization, and Nov. 29, 1802, was admitted into the Union as a State, with its seat of government at Chillicothe.

TERRITORY OF INDIANA ORGANIZED.

After Ohio was separated under a territorial government, the remainder continued to be governed as the Northwestern Territory until 1802, when the Territory of Indiana was organized with William Henry Harrison as Governor. In 1803 the first legislature of Indiana Territory assembled at Vincennes. Illinois then being a part of Indiana Territory, St. Clair county sent three representatives.

TERRITORY OF ILLINOIS ORGANIZED.

By an act of Congress, approved Feb. 3, 1809, Illinois was separated from Indiana, and provision made for organizing a Territorial Government.

Hon. Ninian Edwards, Chief Justice of Kentucky, was appointed by President Madison to be the first Governor of the Territory of Illinois. The government was organized by Nathaniel Pope, Territorial Secretary, April 28, 1809. Governor Edwards arrived at Kaskaskia early in June, and on the 11th of that month took the oath of office. He was Governor during the whole of the territorial existence of Illinois. His first commission was dated March 7, 1809; re-appointed Nov. 12, 1812; again re-appointed, Jan. 16, 1816. Gov. Edwards was the father of Hon. Ninian W. Edwards and Hon. B. S. Edwards, among the oldest and most respected citizens of Springfield.

From 1809 to 1812, all the legislation was done "By authority of the Governor and Judges." They did not enact laws, but only selected from the territorial laws of Indiana and from the State of Kentucky such as were suitable to the situation, and declared them to be laws of the territory of Illinois.

The first election in Illinois was held March 14, 1812, by order of Governor Edwards, for the purpose of ascertaining whether or not the people desired to take part in the government, by a territorial organization. The result of the election was favorable to the change. An election was then ordered to take place Oct. 9, 10, 11, for the purpose of choosing a delegate to Congress and members of the Legislature.

The first legislative body in the Territory assembled at Kaskaskia, Nov. 25, 1812. From that time to 1818, all business was done in the name of the "Legislative Council and House of Representatives." That body assembled in December, annually, until the organization of the State government.

STATE GOVERNMENT ORGANIZED.

By an act of Congress, approved April 18, 1818, the people of Illinois were authorized to advance from a territorial to a State government. In August an election was held for State officers and a Representative in Congress. The State was admitted into the Union on the third of December following.

Shadrach Bond, who had been a delegate in Congress from 1811 to 1815, and receiver in the land office from that time until the State was admitted into the Union, was elected the first Governor under the State organization. Ex-Governor Edwards and Jesse B. Thomas were chosen by the legislature to be the first United States Senators.

SPRINGFIELD AND SANGAMON COUNTY.

When Illinois was admitted into the Union, it was composed of thirty-three counties, but Springfield and Sangamon county were unknown.

Towns and cities are born, live and die, subject to the contingencies of birth, life and death, analagous to that of human beings. About the year 1818 an old bachelor by the name of Kelly, emigrated from North Carolina to this State. Mr. Kelly was exceedingly fond of the chase, and in prospecting for good hunting grounds, wandered in between two ravines, a couple of miles apart, running in a northwesterly direction and emptying into Spring creek, a tributary of Sangamon river.

The deer with which this country abounded, before the advent of civilization, made their homes in the timber along the large water courses. In the morning they would leave the heavy timber, follow up the ravines, along which the trees became smaller, and finally run out on the open prairie. They would pass the day amid the tall and luxuriant grass, roaming about and grazing at pleasure, and as nightfall approached, return down the ravines, to the places they had left in the morning, each to seek its lair for repose. The deer in passing up and down these ravines, gave Mr. Kelly an opportunity for the full gratification of his ambition for game. It seemed to him so much like a hunter's paradise, that he returned to his old home, and induced two of his brothers, with their families and one or more other families among his acquaintances, to emigrate with him. More families continued to move into the country, and generally settled at long distances from each other, but the principal settlement clustered around the Kelly's.

By an act of the legislature, approved Jan. 30, 1821, the county of Sangamon was formed by taking part from each of the counties of Bond and Madison. It embraced what are now the counties of Sangamon, Logan, Mason, Menard, Tazewell, Cass and parts of Morgan, Christian, McLean, Marshall, Woodford and Putnam.

By an act of Dec. 23, 1824, the boundaries of the county were reduced, but it still extended to the Illinois river, and included the present counties of Sangamon and Menard, with parts of Christian, Logan and Mason.

By an act of the General Assembly,

approved Feb. 15, 1839, the counties of Menard, Logan and Dane were established. The whole of Menard and a part of what is Logan, Mason and Dane, were taken from Sangamon, reducing it to the present limits. The name of Dane has since been changed to Christian.

The act of Jan. 30, 1824, which provided for organizing the county of Sangamon, created a board of three commissioners, whose first duty was declared to be the selection of a temporary seat of justice. The first meeting of the commissioners, was held at the house of John Kelly, April 3, 1821. Without coming to a decision, the board adjourned to meet at the same place on the 10th of the month. Before their next meeting, by their investigations they became aware of the fact, that the Kelly neighborhood was the only place in all the county, large as it was, where enough families could be found in the vicinity of each other, to board and lodge the members of the court and those who would be likely to attend its sessions. The commissioners met pursuant to adjournment, on the 10th and fixed upon a location. In their report, after discussing the questions pro and con, with regard to the different localities, they came to the following conclusion: "Therefore, we the undersigned, county commissioners, do certify that we, after full examination of the situation, of the present population of said county, have fixed and designated a certain point in the prairie, near John Kelly's field, on the waters of Spring creek, at a stake set, marked Z. P., as the temporary seat of justice for said county, and further agree that said county seat be known by the name of SPRINGFIELD." The initials on the stake were doubtless, those of Zecharia Peter, who was one of the commissioners and the first county surveyor. The first court ever held in the county, was at the house of John Kelly, and commenced May 1, 1821, just half a century ago.

COURT HOUSES IN SANGAMON COUNTY.

The point chosen for the new county buildings, is now the northwest corner of Jefferson and Second streets. A log Court House and Jail was built there in the latter part of 1821. The Court House was built under contract for $84 00. I fail to find that there was any Court House Ring formed, or that there were any persons about who were disappointed because they could not have a hand in spending the money, shouting steal! steal!

An incident said to have occurred about this time, will illustrate the disposition of the early settlers to give an amusing turn to passing events. An attorney at the bar, violated the rules of decorum as understood by the Judge. His honor, ever bearing in mind the dignity of the court, ordered the lawyer to be arrested, and sent him to jail for a few hours. On repairing to the Court House next morning, the Judge, attorneys and others, were surprised to find the court in session, before the hour to which it had adjourned. A large calf was on the platform, usually occupied by the Judge, and a flock of geese, cooped up in the jury box. The attorney who had been in jail the day before, was inside the bar; bowing first to the calf, and then to the geese; he commenced his pleading,—"May it please the Court, and you gentlemen of the Jury."

The $84 00 Court House did well for a time, but aristocratic feelings began to prevail, and we find the result in a contract, on file at the office of the County Clerk, made in September, 1825, for building another Court House. Log buildings could be no longer tolerated, and this was to be a frame. The contract price was $449 00, but it was too big a thing to let it all in one contract, so the building of the flues was let to another party for $70 00, making a total of $519 00. The old log Court House was sold for $32 00. The new frame Court House was at the northeast corner of Adams and Sixth streets, opposite where the American House now stands.

Only a few years elapsed until the frame Court house was thought to be inadequate to the wants of the people. We find it on record in the county archives that in February, 1830, the county court appointed three agents or commissioners to superintend the erection of a brick Court House. On the third of March, the commissioners reported to the court that they had entered into contracts with two parties. One for the brick work at $4,641, the other for the wood work at $2,200, making a total of $6,841. This edifice was completed early in 1831 and stood in the centre of the public square, where the State House now stands. This old Court House was a square building, two stories high, hip roof, with a cupola rising in the centre.

From the time the brick Court House was erected, all the business of the town collected around the square. When Springfield was selected as the future Capital of the State in 1837, with a pledge to raise $50,000 to assist in building the State House, also to furnish the land upon which to place it, it was not an easy matter to agree upon a location. If land was selected far enough from the existing business to be cheap, then the $50,000 could not be raised; those already in business around the square refused to contribute because the State House being so much larger and more attractive, would draw the business after it, thus injuring the value of their property. After discussing the question in all its bearings, it was found that the only practicable way to settle the question was to demolish the Court House and use the square for the State House. Then those in business around it would contribute to the $50,000 fund to the extent of their ability.

The Court House was accordingly removed, early in 1837, and work on the State House commenced. This square, with the Court House and other buildings on it, were valued at the time at about $16,000.

Having thus summarily disposed of their Court House, and having engaged to do so much towards building the State House, the people of Sangamon Co. were unable to undertake the building of another. To supply the deficiency, the county authorities then rented a building that had been erected for a storehouse by the Hon. Ninian W. Edwards. This building at the west side of Fifth street, five doors north of Washington, was used as a Court House for about ten years. It still belongs to Mr. Edwards and is now receiving some additions and undergoing some alterations and repairs, in order to fit it up for a first-class business house.

After the State. House was built, the $50,000 paid, and the county emerged from the general wreck, accompanying the financial crash of 1837–8, Sangamon county once more began to take measures for erecting another Court House. In the month of February, 1845, a lot of ground was purchased at the southeast corner of Washington and Sixth streets, preparatory to building. April 22, 1845, a contract was made by the county commissioners for building the new Court House, according to plans and specifications previously adopted. The new building was to cost $9,680, and to be paid for in county orders. It was completed according to contract and is yet used as the Court House of Sangamon county.

In giving the prices paid for all these Court Houses, no attention has been given to the cost of the land, but the buildings only.

This latter building will be used for the business of the county, until the completion of the New State House, and the old one is vacated by the State, after which that will be the Court House of Sangamon county.

FIRST SURVEY OF PUBLIC LANDS.

The first survey of public lands in Sangamon county, took place in the year 1821. Rev. John M. Peck, in his Pioneer History of Illinois, says that Springfield was laid out in February, 1822, referring no doubt to Calhoun, which was the name first given to the first plat of what is now a part of Springfield. It is in the northwestern part of the city. The first sale of public lands in Sangamon county, took place Nov. 7, 1823. At that sale the lands were purchased, upon which Calhoun had been laid out. Four different parties entered each a quarter, of as many sections, cornering together. The town plat of Calhoun was recorded December 5, 1823.

An act of the legislature, approved December 23, 1824, provided for fixing the boundary of the county, and named commissioners who should permanently locate the county seat. A proviso in the law forbid its being located unless at least thirty-five acres of land was donated on the spot. The commissioners assembled March 18, 1825, and confirmed the former location. Forty-two acres were at once donated by Elijah Iles and Pascal Enos.

Between the time of the temporary and permanent location of the county seat, at an election for members of the legislature, two opposing candidates went before the people, on the merits of two localities for the permanent county seat. I. H. Pugh was the candidate for Springfield, and William S. Hamilton—a son of the great Alexander Hamilton—represented Sangamo, a beautiful site for a town, on the banks of the Sangamon river, about seven miles west, bearing a little north from Springfield. Mr. Hamilton was elected, but Pugh went to Vandalia as a lobby member and succeeded in having commissioners appointed who were favorable to Springfield.

After fixing the location, the commissioners laid out the land that had been donated into lots, making the streets correspond with those of Calhoun. The name of Calhoun soon ceased to be used, except in the conveyance of lots.

FIRST LEGISLATION FOR SPRINGFIELD.

The first legislation on the part of the State, with reference to Springfield was approved February 9, 1827. By this act the court of county commissioners were required to appoint street commissioners for the town, and levy a tax for improving the same.

An act of the General Assembly, approved February 12, 1831, was a general law for the incorporation of towns. April 2, 1832, Springfield was incorporated under that law. October 18, 1832, the county court ordered a re-survey of the town, in order to adjust the discrepancies between the plats of Calhoun and Springfield. The survey was made and acknowledged June 18, 1833, and recorded November 9, 1836.

By the act of the General Assembly of Illinois, approved February 3, 1840, a city charter was granted to Springfield. This law provided for an election to be held on the first Monday in April, to adopt or reject the proposed charter. The election was held on the 6th day of the month and the charter was adopted. April 20, 1840, the first election was held for city officers.

STATE CAPITOLS.

The building which was used as a territorial capitol was a French structure, in the primitive style of architecture. Judge Caton, in his oration at the laying of the corner stone of the new State House, October 5, 1868, described it by saying: "It was a rough building in the centre of a square in the village of Kaskaskia, the ancient seat of the western empire for more than one hundred and fifty years. The body of this building was of uncut limestone, the gables and roof of the gambrel style, of unpainted boards and shingles, with dormer windows. The lower floor, a long, cheerless room, was fitted up for the House, whilst the Council sat in the small chamber above. This venerable building was, during the French occupancy of the country, prior to 1763, the headquarters of the military commandant. Thirty years ago the house was a mass of ruins, and to-day, probably, there is not a stone left to designate the spot where it stood."

During the whole territorial existence of Illinois, the building just described was the Capitol, and the State Government was inaugurated there also.

The State Constitution of 1818 required the General Assembly to petition Congress for a grant of land, upon which to locate the seat of government for the State. In the event of the prayer of the petitioners being granted, a town was to be laid out on said land, which town should be the seat of government for the State for twenty years. The prayer of the petitioners was granted. "At the session of 1819 in Kaskaskia, five commissioners were appointed to select the land appropriated by Congress for the State Capital." They made their selection further up the Kaskaskia river. The ground fixed upon was covered with an exceedingly heavy growth of timber. Having agreed upon the place, the commissioners united their intellectual faculties in a gigantic effort to select a name that should be sufficiently high-sounding and euphonious to attract the attention of the whole country. Governor Ford, in his history of Illinois, gives the following humorous account of the way it was done:

"Tradition says that a wag, who was present, suggested to the commissioners that the "Vandals" were a powerful nation of Indians, who once inhabited the banks of the Kaskaskia river, and that "Vandalia," derived from the name, would perpetuate the memory of that extinct but renowned people. The suggestion pleased the commissioners, the name was adopted, and they thus proved that the cognomen of their new city—if they were fit representatives of their constituents—would better illustrate the character of the modern than the ancient inhabitants of the country."

As soon as the town was laid out, the timber was cut away and a two story frame building erected, on the square set apart for the State Capitol. The edifice was placed on a rough stone foundation, in the centre of the square, and was of very rude workmanship. The lower floor was for the House of Representatives, and the upper divided into two rooms, the largest one for the Senate and the smaller for the office of secretary of state. The auditor and treasurer occupied detached buildings. The archives of the State were removed from Kaskaskia to Vandalia in December, 1820.

This wooden State House was burned

and a much larger one built of brick, on the same ground. The brick building is now used by Fayette county as a Court House, Vandalia being the county seat.

The rapidity with which emigration filled up the northern part of the State rendered it apparent, long before the expiration of the time, that it would be necessary to move the Capital farther north, and as early as 1833 the question began to be agitated in the General Assembly.

From the time Sangamon county was organized and Springfield fixed as the county seat, it grew steadily though not rapidly. Among the new comers there was an unusually large number of men of more than ordinary talents, many of whom afterwards acquired National distinction. Among these may be mentioned Abraham Lincoln, Stephen A. Douglas, E. D. Baker, and many others who are yet living. When the question of relocating the Cap itol came up, Sangamon county was very ably represented.

In the Legislature of 1836-7 she had two Senators and seven Representatives, who were not only men of talents, but persistent workers. They were the most remarkable delegation from any one county to the General Assembly, for the reason that they were much taller than the average of human stature. I have just learned from one of the number—Hon. Ninian W. Edwards—who is yet living in this city, that some of them were a little less and some a little more than six feet, but that their combined height was exactly fifty-four feet. For this reason they were then and are yet spoken of as the "Long Nine." The names of those in the Senate were, *A. G. Herndon and Job Fletcher; in the House, *Abraham Lincoln, Ninian W. Edwards, *John Dawson, *Andrew McCormick, *Daniel Stone, W. F. Elkin and Robert L. Wilson. One or two were as tall, but none taller, than Abraham Lincoln, who was just six feet and two inches. Those marked with a star are all deceased.

The removal of the Capital was a foregone conclusion. The members of the Legislature found much fault with Vandalia, because they were fed almost entirely on prairie chickens and venison—very common articles of food at the time, although they are considered luxuries now; but the law makers wanted something better, or at any rate a change. Perhaps no other place would have done better; but experience proves that when a body of Legislators wish to find fault with a town, it is easy to raise pretexts. There was, however, a real necessity for moving the seat of government further north, as the tide of emigration set steadily in that direction, and the means of travel were confined almost entirely to stage coaches and riding on horse back.

The people of Illinois were, at that time, almost crazy on the subject of internal improvements. Not more than one in ten thousand of them had ever seen a railroad, but they had heard of them, and thought the prairies of Illinois the best place in the world to build them. Charters were granted for them in nearly all parts of the State. The "Long Nine" were a unit for securing the State Capital, consequently did not jeopardize it by putting in claims for other improvements. The result was the passage of "An act permanently to locate the seat of government for the State of Illinois," which was approved at Vandalia, February 25, 1837. This law provided for a joint session of the two houses on the 28th of the same month, to select a situation. An appropriation of fifty thousand dollars was made, to commence building the State House. The law also declared that no place should be chosen unless its citizens contributed at least $50,000 to aid in the work, and not less than two acres of land, as a site for the Capitol. When the two houses assembled on the 28th, it was decided that Springfield should be the permanent seat of government of the State of Illinois.

"A supplemental act was passed March 3d, authorizing the commissioners of Sangamon county to convey the land, as a site for the new edifice, to the State. It also named three commissioners, who were authorized and instructed to superintend the work. It was expected that the new Capitol would be completed in time for the first meeting of the Legislature in Springfield, which was fixed for the special session of 1839–40. Finding that this could not be done, the Second Presbyterian church,on Fourth street—the old building by the side of that in which the House of Representatives for 1871 transacted its business—was secured as Representative Hall, the Methodist church for the Senate Chamber, and the Episcopal church for the Supreme court. The first was and is yet quite a commodious brick edifice; the two latter, small, wooden buildings, have long since disappeared as churches. The Legislature first convened at Springfield, in special session, December 9, 1839.

OFFERS TO RELEASE SPRINGFIELD OF THE $50,000.

It is worthy of remark just here that the clause requiring $50,000 to be paid by the town where the Capital should be located was inserted to secure the vote of one man.

It was thought by many of the membersto be unreasonable to require a little town of eleven hundred inhabitants, struggling with all the disadvantages of a new country—the privations of which cannot be realized by those living in these days of railroads—and no less a personage than the Hon. Stephen A. Douglas, then a member from Morgan county, proposed to bring in a bill before the close of that session, releasing Springfield from the payment of the $50,000 pledged. The sterling honesty of Abraham Lincoln manifested itself here as on all other proper occasions. He interposed his objections, although he felt that the offer was made in good faith and with the most kindly feeling, but insisted that the money should be paid to the full extent. In this he was supported by every one of the "Long Nine."

Arrangements were made to pay the money in three installments. The two first payments were made without any great difficulty; but the third one pressed more heavily, as the financial crash that swept over the whole United States, while the new State House was in course of construction, impoverished many. Under these circumstances it became necessary to borrow the money, to make the last payment, from the State Bank of Illinois.

THE NOTE OF ONE HUNDRED AND ONE CITIZENS.

If any citizen of the State, visiting the city, would like to know how it was done, he can, by stepping into the Ridgley National Bank, see in a frame, over the outside desk, the original note, making $16,666 67, payable to the State Bank of Illinois, twelve months after date, with semi-annual interest, at the rate of six per cent. per annum until paid. It is dated March 22, 1838, and signed by one hundred and one citizens of Springfield.

The money thus obtained was used in the purchase of Internal Improvement scrip or stock, which was paid into the State treasury. Thus the last installment of the $50,000 was paid in the State's own evidences of indebtedness.

Many names are on this paper, of men whom the world have known only to love and respect. Here I find the names of E. D. Baker and A. Lincoln, as close together as it would be convenient to write them. I might name many more who have made their influence felt for the right and been honored in return.

The first payment on this note was $500 interest, Sept. 22, 1838, exactly six months from date. Then there are a great number of credits, the last being April 23, 1844. By the time it was paid, principal and interest amounted to nearly $18,000. Between the date of this note and the time it was paid, the State Bank of Illinois failed, and its affairs went into liquidation. Some of the payments on the note were made in the depreciated paper of the Bank, for which it had received par value when it was paid out. This has been charged against Springfield as a breach of good faith. The charge is entirely unjust. If one business man owes another money, and the creditor fails, it is considered both morally and legally right for the debtor to pay the creditor in his own paper, although it may be worthless in commercial transactions. Many of the men whose names were on the note, doubtless lost money by the failure of the bank, and it was no more than right that they should save themselves as far as possible in this transaction; so I submit that the pledges of Springfield and Sangamon county were as faithfully redeemed as if all had been paid in gold.

PUBLIC FESTIVAL.

Early in 1837 a public festival was held in Springfield, in honor of the legislation for the removal of the Capital. Toasts and speeches followed the dinner. Among many others, I find the following, by Abraham Lincoln, Esq.:

"All our Friends—They are too numerous to mention now, individually, while there is no one of them who is not too dear to be forgotten or neglected."

Immediately following this was one by S. A. Douglas, Esq.

"The last Winter's Legislation—May its results prove no less beneficial to the whole State than they have to our town."

There is a tradition here that something stronger than water was used in drinking the toasts on that occasion, as no man could be found, after the festival, that could tell who made the last speech.

LAYING CORNER STONE OF THE FIRST STATE HOUSE.

Soon after the adjournment of the Legislature, the commissioners entered upon the discharge of their duties, and July 4, 1837, the corner stone was laid with grand civic and military demonstrations. After the corner stone had been lowered to its place in the wall, it was mounted by E. D. Baker — afterwards United States Senator, and the lamented Colonel of Ball's Bluff memory—who delivered one of the most thrilling and eloquent speeches, for which he was so famous. It was estimated that the building would cost $130,000, but $240,000 was expended before it was completed according to the original design. Deducting the $50,000 paid by Springfield, leaves $190,000 as the cost of that building to the State.

When the State House was completed, it was looked upon with wonder and admiration by the people, who regarded it as a model of architectural beauty. It is built of lime stone, which is composed almost entirely of fossils. It was taken from a quarry seven or eight miles south of Springfield, and hauled by ox teams to the place selected for the building. The size of the edifice was thought to be so enormous that it would answer the purposes of the State for all time to come. It was, for the time, really a commodious and handsome building, but now it will make a very moderate Court House for Sangamon county. From the time the State House was built here, until the breaking out of the great rebellion, the growth of Illinois was beyond anything that the early settlers could have imagined.

BUILDING THE LELAND HOTEL.

Springfield, as the Capital, had not grown in anything like its due proportion to the State, but during the rebellion its growth was more rapid. At the close of the war, the hotel accommodations of Springfield were inadequate to the demands of the public. In order to supply the deficiency, a joint stock company was organized, and in 1866 the magnificent Leland Hotel was erected and furnished at a cost of $350,000. It was opened to the public, on the assembling of the Legislature, Jan. 1, 1867.

MOVEMENTS FOR A NEW STATE HOUSE.

For several years prior to this time, it was apparent to all business men and politicians, who had occasion to visit Springfield, that the building of a new State House could not be much longer delayed. The State had outgrown its public buildings so much that its records were unsafe, and many branches of its official business had to be transacted in rented buildings, where much of its valuable property was exposed at all times to the dangers of destruction by fire. There began to be intimations thrown out that when the question did come up for legislation, other important towns would endeavor to bring influences to bear in favor of re-location and removal.

These difficulties were foreseen and understood by the citizens of Springfield, and although it was felt to be an obstacle to the growth of the city, yet all seemed disposed to put off the evil day as long as possible. During the summer of 1866, Hon. J. C. Conkling became a candidate for a seat in the lower branch of the General Assembly, with the view of making the question of building a new State House a prominent subject before the Legislature, if elected. Mr. Conkling went before the people upon this question and the politics of the day, and was elected, although his opponent was friendly to the move for a new State House also. The election was held in November, 1866.

Hon. John S. Bradford was Mayor of Springfield at the time, and in consequence of the general feeling on the State House question, he, soon after the State election, sent out private invitations, to some forty or fifty of the most prominent business men, to meet him on a certain evening in a hall, named in the invitation. When they were assembled, Mayor Bradford was called on to preside and state the object of the meeting. He informed them that it was to hold a consultation with reference to bringing the subject of building a new Capitol for the State, before the General Assembly, for its action at the approaching session. After the delivery of a brief address by the Mayor, a general interchange of views followed, when it was found that the feeling was almost unanimous in favor of action. By subsequent meetings and consultations with the board of Supervisors for Sangamon county and the city authorities of Springfield, those two organizations were ready to purchase the old State House for the use of the county and city, in the event of the General Assembly deciding to erect a new one.

LAW PROVIDING FOR BUILDING A NEW CAPITOL.

Accordingly, when the Legislature assembled, Mr. Conkling presented a bill providing for the erection of a new State Capitol at Springfield, and laid it before the House of Representatives early in the session. It was referred to the committee on public buildings; and after remaining in their hands several weeks, during which time some changes were made, the principal one being an increase of the amount to be paid for the old State House. It was reported back to the House, with the unanimous recommendation that it be adopted. It passed both Houses, and was approved by Gov. R. J. Oglesby, Feb. 25, 1867, with a supplementary act two days later.

This law provided, first, for the conveyance by the Governor, of the public square, containing two and a half acres of land, with the State House upon it, to Sangamon county and the city of Springfield, in consideration of $200,000, to be paid to the State of Illinois, and for the further consideration that the city and county cause to be conveyed to the State a certain piece of land, described by metes and bounds, in the bill, and containing between eight and nine acres, upon which to erect the new State House. This bill also provides that the State shall have the use of the old State House until the new one is completed. The land was secured at a cost to the city of $70,000, and conveyed to the State; the $200,000 was paid by the county, and that amount, with $250,000 more to be drawn from the State treasury, making $450,000, was appropriated to commence the work.

It is proper here to state that the $200,000, paid nominally for the old State House, was really in consideration that a new one was to be built. The people of Sangamon county would now much prefer to re-convey it to the State, if they could have refunded the $200,000, with the $80,000 interest, that the money has been worth during that time; then they could build a Court House much more to their liking, for a much smaller amount of money.

It is a matter in which the people have a right to feel an honest pride, that while other towns and cities in different parts of the State have made liberal offers to secure the location of some State institution, only to evade its provisions, and in the end leave the State to make up their deficiencies, Springfield and Sangamon county have redeemed every pledge they have made to the people of the State. Upon this subject they invite the closest scrutiny.

In the law, seven men were named as commissioners, to superintend the erection of the new State House, and disburse the funds appropriated for that purpose. They were instructed to advertise for plans and specifications, for thirty days, in two daily papers each, in Springfield and Chicago, and one each, in Philadelphia and New York. After waiting three months they were to notify the committees on public buildings as provided by law, who were to unite with the commissioners in adopting a design. The commissioners were to be governed by the plan so adopted, and the total cost of the building was not to exceed $3,000,000. March 5, 1867, they advertised "Notice to Architects," offering $3,000 to the architect whose design should be adopted for the new State House, and asking for plans and specifications to be submitted for their inspection.

EFFORTS TO NULLIFY THE LAW AND THEIR FAILURE.

A writ of *quo warranto*—or an inquiry as to their right or authority to act—was issued against the commissioners, from the Superior Court of Chicago, May 13, 1867, on the relation of Mathew Laflin, and judgment of ouster was entered. The commissioners appealed to the Supreme Court, and the decision was reversed at Ottawa in September of that year. The commissioners having advertised for proposals before the commencement of the suit, and having named the 15th of July as the time for inspecting the designs, and being deprived of the power to act by the decision of the Superior Court of Chicago, placed both themselves and architects in an awkward position. The Supreme Court, however, came to their relief by giving special permission to the commissioners to call to their assistance the committees on public buildings as provided by law, and the inspection took place as previously intended, on the 15th of July, in the Senate Chamber at Springfield. A large number of designs were submitted to their inspection, and after mature deliberation, that presented by J. C. Cochrane of Chicago, was adopted.

The commissioners being compelled to remain inactive until after the meeting of the Supreme Court in September, it was too late in the season to do anything more than prepare for active business the next year. Their first act after the decision of the Supreme Court reinstating them, was on the 8th of November, when they issued an advertisement for sealed proposals to do the excavating, and furnish certain descriptions of stone.

January 14, 1868, John C. Cochrane was appointed architect and superintendent, and a contract entered into for that purpose. January 18, a contract was made with N. Strott, of Springfield, for the excavation ; and January 20th, with R. W. McClaughry & Co., of Hancock county, for stone to build the foundation. Broken stone for concrete was purchased ready delivered, of J. J. & W. H. Mitchell, of Alton. March 25th, a contract was made with Barnard & Gowen, of Chicago, to do the mason work.

MAGNITUDE OF THE WORK.

The magnitude of the enterprise may be inferred from the fact that the parties who furnished the foundation stone, gave security in the penal sum of $550,000 for the performance of contract, and those who do the mason work a penal sum of $200,000. Excavating was commenced early in the spring, but owing to the excessive rains, the ground was not in a proper condition to commence laying stone until June 11, 1868. From that time until cold weather put a stop to it, the work was prosecuted vigorously, and a part of the foundation was brought to a level with the surface during the month of September.

LAYING CORNER STONE.

The Grand Master of Masons for the State of Illinois was invited by the commissioners to assemble the craft for the purpose of laying the corner stone of the New State House, with the imposing ceremonials of the order. The invitation was accepted, and October 5 set apart as the time at which it was to take place. A stone was prepared, eight feet long, four feet wide and three feet deep, with a recess for receiving such articles as it was thought desirable to deposit. A catalogue of them would fill one of these pages.

The day was bright and cheerful, and the procession the largest that had ever been seen at the capital of the State, except at the obsequies of President Lincoln in May, 1865. Masons were present from all parts of the State, of all degrees, from Master Mason to Knight Templar. After the corner stone had been tested by the implements of the order, and pronounced well formed, true and trusty, it was placed in its proper position at the northeast corner of the building. An eloquent oration was then delivered by the Hon. John D. Caton, of Ottawa. The ceremonials having closed, the craft and others present were called from labor to refreshment, and all repaired to the "Rink" to partake of a sumptuous collation prepared by the Lelands. After dinner the multitude dispersed to their homes, to treasure up the memories of the day as one of the most pleasant waymarks of their lives.

DESCRIPTION OF THE NEW STATE HOUSE.

Without regard to such technicalities as would be pleasing to architects, I shall endeavor to describe the edifice, in such language as will be most easily understood by the common reader. The ground plan is in the form of a great cross, and the superstructure is in the style called the classic order of architecture. It so blends the ancient and modern art of building as to secure the greatest strength and solidity and yet preserve an exterior appearance so light and airy as to be very pleasant to the eye. The grand outlines are, total length from north to south, 359 feet, exclusive of the porticos, which adds twenty feet to each end. From east to west it is 266 feet, with twenty feet additional in the grand portico at the east end, which is the principal front. There is an excavation under ground of ten feet depth, throughout the entire area. It is designed by the architect for the heating apparatus, the storage of fuel and other heavy articles. So much of the floor as is used, is to be covered with concrete.

The next above this is the FIRST STORY; it is nineteen feet high, and entirely above ground. The floor of this story is supported by brick arches; and in the halls the arches are double, one being two feet below the other, to form viaducts to supply the rooms with fresh air. A layer of concrete covers the entire area of the arches, and upon this, imbedded in cement, is laid the marble floors throughout.

On this floor we find private rooms for the Judges of the Supreme Court and committee rooms. The largest portion of this floor is devoted to the storage of stationery, printing paper, and all articles connected with or used in any other part of the building. One of these rooms is for the storage of Geological specimens, and another for geological artists. One or more is for the Adjutant General's office and museum. This story, in addition to the windows on all sides, is lighted by a glass ceiling in the centre, which forms the floor of the Rotunda above.

Above this is the PRINCIPAL STORY, which is twenty-two feet and a half from floor to ceiling. On this floor is the Main Corridor, running the entire length of the building from north to south, and the Grand Corridor crossing it at right angles under the dome, and extending across the building from east to west. The Main Corridor is 359 feet long, twenty-four feet wide and twenty-two and a half feet high.

The sides of the Main Corridor will be finished with marble pilasters projecting from the walls, thus forming panels. The

View of the New State House.

entire walls on both sides, consisting of pilasters with their caps and bases, panels and their borders, and door finish, are all to be of variagated marble, and the ceiling to be frescoed. The Grand Corridor, extending from the east portico to the Grand Stairway in the western wing, is so called in consideration of its great width—thirty-two feet—and because the pilasters are more massive and the finish more elaborate than in the Main Corridor.

The rooms on the floor described are to be used as follows: Governor's reception and private rooms; office of the Secretary of State; of the Treasurer of State, and of the Auditor of Public Accounts; Superintendent of Public Instruction; Superintendent of Public Instruction's library; law library; State document library; Attorney General's office; supreme court room; supreme court clerk's office; four massive stone fire-proof vaults, and the State Treasurer's burglar-proof safe. The State Geologist's museum, is just over the State Geologist's store room in the first story, with which it is connected by a private stairway; State Geologist's office. With all these, there are the necessary water closets, wash rooms, private offices, and the Grand Stairway which leads to the story above. This flight is to be made of Tennessee marble, the steps each sixteen feet long.

The floors of this story are supported

by wrought iron beams, properly braced with angle irons, all well secured with rivets. The spaces between the wrought iron beams are filled with brick arches, the whole of which is covered with concrete, having wooden strips imbedded, to hold the wooden floors, in the rooms only. The floors in the halls and corridors are all marble, chequered by alternate squares of different colors.

The principal entrance is at the east side, by an immense flight of stone steps, seventy-three feet wide, landing in a Grand Portico.

We will ascend the front steps, enter the east portico, pass along the Grand Corridor, over the glass floor in the rotunda, and continue west, to the foot of the grand stairway, which we ascend, to half the height of the story, then turn about, either to the right or left, and ascend to the SECOND PRINCIPAL STORY. The floor of this story is constructed exactly as the one described below. Keep in mind that the entire edifice retains the form of a grand cross—first story, principal story, and second principal story. It is the floor of the latter on which we are now standing.

This story is forty-five feet from floor to ceiling. Let us enter the north angle or arm of the cross. Here we find the Senate Chamber, sixty-two by seventy-five feet, with the desk of the presiding officer at the north side. In the extreme north end of this wing, we find rooms properly arranged for the speaker, chief lerk, enrolling and engrossing clerks, sergeant at-arms, post office, and folding room; with corridors on the east and west sides.

We will now pass out south, around the rotunda, and across the corridor into the Hall of the House of Representatives, in the southern angle of the building. This hall is sixty-six by one hundred feet, with speaker's desk at the west side. The desks here, as in the Senate Chamber, are in a semi-circular form. Here we find, under somewhat different arrangements, rooms attached, for the same offices as those connected with the Senate Chamber. In both halls there are cloak rooms, wash rooms and water closets conveniently attached. Both are lighted in the day time, principally through the roof.

The east wing has rooms for the Canal Commissioners, and committee rooms, with cloak and other necessary rooms attached. Between these rooms and the rotunda there is a lobby 26 x 104 feet, extending across the wing from north to south.

The west wing has rooms for the State library, the librarian, a reading room, and an audience room each, for the Senate and House of Representatives.

The Senate Chamber and Representatives Hall have each a gallery, extending around three sides, half way from floor to ceiling. A portion of the gallery in each house is set apart for the use of reporters of the press. On a level with the galleries, a floor extends over all the office rooms connected with both houses, the Governor's rooms, State library, reception rooms, and all except the two legislative halls. This floor is divided into a great number of small rooms, for the use of committees of both houses, and is designated the GALLERY STORY.

To impress it on the mind, I will here recapitulate, that the body of the edifice above ground consists of the FIRST STORY, PRINCIPAL STORY, SECOND PRINCIPAL STORY, and GALLERY STORY.

The roof on all the wings is of the Mansard style, covered with slate on the sides and copper on top. Above all this rises the stately DOME, surmounted by a lantern with a ball on the pinnacle, 320 feet from the natural surface of the earth, being forty-three feet higher than the Capitol at Washington. The lantern is sixteen feet wide, and twenty-four feet from bottom to top. The frame work is of iron and the sides of glass. The floor of the lantern will be 280 feet above the surface of the earth. An iron stairway ascending inside the Dome, will afford access to the lantern. The means of communicating between the Basement Story and the Legislative Halls will be by the Grand Stairway and two other public and three private stairways.

In addition to this there will be two steam hoisting apparatus or elevators, by means of which persons can ascend or descend, from one to another of the floors, by simply stepping on and off a platform.

For heating and ventilating the building, there will be ten boilers, forty-eight inches in diameter and twelve feet long. A steam engine of twenty horse power will be used for running the elevator and a fan twelve feet in diameter, to produce sufficient circulation of air to ventilate the building in a proper manner. There will be 163,500 lineal feet of pipe, used to conduct the steam to all parts of the building.

The principal material used in the edifice is cut stone. Of this there will be nearly three-quarters of a million cubic feet, including the foundation. About one-half of the stone is finely dressed or planed. This does not include the marble, of which there is an enormous quantity. In addition to the stone in the walls there will be about twenty millions of brick. Of wrought iron there will be 2,414,101 pounds, or 1,207 tons; and of cast iron 3,673,456 pounds, or 1,836½ tons.

The Rotunda is 76 feet in diameter. From the glass floor, where the Grand and Main corridors cross each other, to the fresco painting, just beneath the Dome, it will be 217 feet without any obstruction to the view whatever.

The three Porticos, at the north, south, and east sides, are to have ten columns, each. These columns are to be 45 feet high, without the plinth block, which is four feet high. The base and cap pieces are to be cut separate; the two make nine feet of the height. Deduct this from forty-five, leaves thirty-six feet as the heighth and four and a half feet diameter, as the dimensions of the columns. Thirty of these are to be cut in single pieces each, from stone in the quarry—if any such can be found.

Let us take our position in front of the east Portico. It is ninety feet wide. From each of the front corners rises a turret, to the heighth of 132 feet. That on the right, or to the north, is to be surmounted by a statue of Lincoln, and the one on the left, or to the south, by a statue of Douglas. This, as I have already stated, is the Principal Front or entrance.

I have thus described, from the working drawings and the book of specifications of Cochrane & Piquenard, superintending architects, the merest outline of the new Capitol of Illinois, now in course of construction, as it will appear when completed. Let us see what has been done towards carrying out the designs laid down on the trestle board.

WORK COMPLETED.

The excavation for the foundation on which the great DOME is to rest, is 25 feet below the natural surface of the ground, and at the bottom is a solid ledge of stone. The area is circular, and is 92½ feet in diameter. The foundation was commenced by covering the entire space, to an average depth of six feet, with concrete, that is, broken stone, cement, clean, sharp sand, and water. This concrete receives the heavy stone walls of an average of 17 feet in thickness, till brought to a level with the first floor, which is 24 feet above the concrete. These walls are not made of heavy stone on the outside and filled in with small ones, but they are all large—some of them two, three, and four tons weight, each. Think of the thickness of the walls, standing on a solid ledge of limestone, and perhaps you can comprehend their solidity.

The excavation for the outer walls, around the entire building, is twelve feet beneath the surface and nine feet wide. The walls are commenced with two feet depth of concrete all over the bottom. They are eight feet and eight inches wide at the bottom, and run up, with offsets, to six feet three inches at the ground line. Parts of the walls are seven feet nine inches at the bottom, tapered to five feet four inches; and yet other portions ten feet and eleven inches at the bottom, and eight feet six inches at the top or natural surface of the ground. The stones in all the foundation are large; not a single one is put in place by hand—they are all moved by steam derricks. One of these machines will take a stone of many tons weight, lift it from the ground, swing it to its place on the wall, and lay it down as easy and gently as a child would take a peach from the floor and lay it on a table.

The foundation was commenced by laying the first stone June 11, 1868, and finished in August, 1869. This includes the foundation for the Dome, and the outer walls around the entire building, 266 by 359 feet, with all the buttresses on the outside, and the inside walls and piers. The superstructure to rise on these walls is to be of heavy stone, with brick backing. To the top of the, First Story, which is twenty-five feet above the ground line, they are five feet thick. *All the walls are now completed to that height.* Viewed from all sides now, it begins to disclose its vast proportions.

From the top of the basement story to the cornice, sixty feet, the walls are to be four feet thick. The brick backing is so constructed as to make them hollow, for the purpose of keeping the interior dry.

W. D. Clark is the assistant superintendent, under the architects. He has done the civil engineering also, having set every stake and laid every line.

A great outcry has been made by some parties that the work was defective. Those who make such charges are either ignorant of what they say or write, or they have some less worthy object in view than to subserve the interests of the State. To those who know Mr. Clark, such a charge seems utterly absurd. They would be no more surprised to hear that he had put his hand in the fire without an object, than to learn that he had permitted a piece of defective material or workmanship to enter into the construction of the edifice.

The entire outer surface of the building, below the Mansard, will be planed Illinois limestone. It is taken from the quarries near Joliet. By a law, enacted in 1869, the work of preparing the stone is confined to the convicts in the State penitentiary. The contractors have, at all times, promptly discharged their obligations.

EPITOME OF THE LEGISLATION FOR THE NEW STATE HOUSE.

The laws of February 25 and 27, 1867, to provide for the erection of a new State House, appropriated $450,000 to begin the work; declared that the total cost should not exceed $3,000,000; named seven commissioners and one secretary to carry out the law; limited the amount of expenditures and liabilities they should incur within the amount appropriated; and delared that everything in excess of that should be deemed unlawful.

Laws of March 11 and 27, 1869, legislated the seven commissioners and secretary out of office; provided for the appointment of three commissioners, by the Governor; ordered that all stone, iron and labor for the new State House that could be procured at the penitentiary, at Joliet, should be obtained there, and at no other place; required the new commissioners to have a full copy of plans, specifications and estimates, made in detail; and when completed, to notify the committees of the Senate and House of

Representatives on public buildings and State library. And said committee were instructed to hold a joint session, to examine the plans, specifications and estimates; and in the event of their being satisfied that the building could be completed within the limit of $3,000,000, in addition to what had already been expended, they were to order the commissioners to proceed; appropriated $650,000, to be used in carrying forward the work on the new State House, but prohibited the use of it until the above conditions were complied with.

Under the law of March 11, 1869, Governor Palmer appointed Jacob Bunn, James C. Robinson and James H. Beveridge, as commissioners to continue the work of constructing the new State House. The board organized April 12, 1869, by electing Jacob Bunn, president, and James H. Beveridge, secretary. The commissioners at once caused detailed plans, specifications and estimates for continuing the work on the new State House, to be prepared by the superintending architects. They notified the committees of the Senate and House of Representatives, and a joint session was held in the Senate Chamber at Springfield, April 27, 1869, and a copy of the plans and specifications was laid before them. At a meeting of the committees, on the 12th of May, it was

"*Resolved*, That the State House commissioners be and they hereby are authorized to complete the foundation of the new State House under existing contracts, and to expend the balance of the appropriation first made, or as much thereof as may be necessary for the purpose."

The work was commenced immediately, and the foundation completed early in August, as previously stated.

The total estimates of the superintending architects, submitted with plans and specifications, amounted to $2,650,885. The joint committee deeming it advisable to have the opinions of parties who were not interested, called to their assistance Augustus Bauer and Asher Carter, architects, and W. C. Deakman, master builder, all of Chicago, and had them make an estimate in detail, according to the same plans and specifications, and their estimate was $2,737,940 86—no greater difference in proportion than two builders would make on almost any piece of work.

The joint committee did not complete their investigations until August 26, 1869. They then ordered the commissioners to go forward with the work according to the plans and specifications, with certain alterations recommended by the superintending architects and master builder. They publicly expressed the belief that it could be finished within the $3,000,000, and that "when completed it would be a beautiful, convenient and permanent structure, worthy of the State."

Thus the best part of another season passed away with such hindrances as prevented the commissioners from prosecuting the work as energetically as they desired to do.

The Convention called by the people of Illinois, for the purpose of framing a new Constitution for the State, recognized the facts that the Capitol had been permanently located at Springfield by legal authority, and that a positive law required the work of all State officers and all legislative enactments to be done at Springfield, as the Capital; and that laws had been passed by two previous legislatures, making large appropriations of money for building a new edifice in which to transact the business of the State; and that a design had been adopted on a scale of grandeur and magnificence in proportion to its weatlh and influence, deemed it wise to insert a clause in the new Constitution to guard against abuses too often practiced in connection with works erected at public expense.

The Constitutional Convention, therefore, inserted under the miscellaneous head, the following:

Section 33. The General Assembly shall not appropriate out of the State treasury, or expend on account of the new Capitol grounds, and construction, completion and furnishing of the State House, a sum exceeding, in the aggregate, three and a half millions of dollars, inclusive of all appropriations heretofore made, without first submitting the proposition for an additional expenditure to the legal voters of the State, at a general election, nor unless a majority of all the votes cast at such election shall be for the proposed additional expenditure."

With this provision in the new Constitution, it was submitted to the people July 2, 1870, and adopted by an overwhelming majority.

The appropriation of Feb. 25, 1867, was $450,000, and that of March 11, 1869, $650,000, making a total of $1,100,000.

The expenditures have been as follows:

From beginning to Dec. 30, 1868	$354,126 12
From Dec. 30, 1868, to March 11, 1869	16,657 07
Total expenditures by first board of seven commissioners	$370,783 19

The board of three commissioners appointed by Governor Palmer, under the law of March 11, 1869, have carried the work forward, and their expenditures—

To Nov. 30, 1869, was	$156,876 76
From Nov. 30, 1869, to Nov. 30, 1870	277,543 13
From Nov. 30, 1870, to Feb. 1, 1871	77.918 79
Total to Feb. 1, 1871	$883,121 87
From Feb. 1 to April 14, 1871	53,096 91
Due for iron on the way from Belgium	12,895 30
Total	$949,114 08

There is due on existing contracts, for materials and for work, enough to bring the total expenditure up to about $1,000,000, leaving about $100,000 of the appropriation of 1869 unexpended.

Early in the session of the General Assembly, which convened Jan. 4, 1871, a bill was introduced in the Senate, appropriating $600,000 to carry on the work of the new State House. It passed that body by a very small number of dissenting votes. In the House of Representatives it was read a first and second time, and ordered to a third reading, but was not reached in the regular order of business, when the Legislature adjourned temporarily, on the 17th of April.

The sessions of the General Assembly being biennial, each alternate year brings, to a large extent, a new class of men together in the legislative halls. The public has been so accustomed to hear of fraud in connection with buildings of this kind, that men coming for the first time, and looking upon the collossal proportions of this edifice, take it for granted that there must be jobs and peculations, and without investigating the subject, there are always some who are ready to cry out, Rings! Rings! Steals! Steals!

By these devices, one of the two years connected with each Legislature has been frittered away from the commencement, and this order of things seems destined to continue. From this cause the year 1867 was one of inactivity; in 1868 work was done; 1869 was one of idleness; 1870 work, and 1871 is likely to be one of idleness also.

The commissioners, Jacob Bunn, James C. Robinson and James H. Beveridge, have passed through two years of investigation out of the four since the work commenced; and in each instance have emerged from the ordeal without the smell of fire upon their garments. Should the present year prove to be one of inactivity, it will be no fault of theirs; and their works are the only vindication they need, concerning which they take pleasure in giving all the information in their power.

The following quotation from the law, which has been strictly complied with in every particular, is a sufficient refutation, in the estimation of all honest men, of the ridiculous charge that Mr. Bunn is using the money appropriated for building the State House, in his banking business:

"The accounts of the expenditures of

said commissioners shall be certified by said commissioners, or a majority of them, *and by the Secretary of State, and approved by the Governor.* The Auditor shall thereupon draw his warrant upon the Treasurer therefor, to be paid out of the fund herein before provided, *in favor of the party to whom the accounts shall be due.*"

It will thus be seen that Mr. Bunn, like all other citizens, cannot receive a dollar of the State House money, except for services rendered or materials furnished, and then only when his bill is allowed by his associates in office, certified by the Secretary of State and approved by the Governor.

It will not be considered exaggeration by any man who has honestly endeavored to obtain correct information on the subject, for me to say that the work on the new State House has been as well done, and the duties of all connected with it as faithfully discharged, as they have been with any similar undertaking on the American continent.

It will be such a magnificent structure and so well adapted to the uses for which it is designed, that the people can afford to be patient. The work is now about one-third done, and if this should prove to be the last year of idleness, it may yet be completed in time to use it in celebrating the first centennial of American Independence. It will be well worthy of such a christening.

Farmers, mechanics and other laboring men—you who do not often leave your homes for a gala day—you will all want to visit the Capitol, at the dedication of the monument to the memory of Abraham Lincoln, for which will take place some time during the coming autumn. It will not be possible for all to come, but those who do, should give themselves time to examine the work on the new State House also; then you will understand the cupidity of those who are endeavoring to have its massive walls torn down and carted over the State, in order to fill their own pockets at your expense.

PROCLAMATION BY THE GOVERNOR.

Since the above was written, Governor Palmer has issued a proclamation, convening the Legislature on the 24th of this month—May. In that proclamation he enumerates thirteen subjects requiring immediate action on the part of the General Assembly. An appropriation for continuing the work on the new State House is one of the subjects named.

EARLY HISTORY OF RAILROAD LEGISLATION IN ILLINOIS.

Illinois appears to have been destined to become a great railroad State, from the time they were introduced into the country. Her law-makers did not wait for them to come by connecting links, from the Atlantic coast, but moved in the matter independent of the States between her and the eastern seaboard.

As early as 1833 the subject of building railroads was introduced into the General Assembly, but no laws were enacted at that time. The first move was a bold one, when we consider the limited amount of capital in the country and that the resources of the State were almost entirely undeveloped. It was :

An act to incorporate the Chicago and Vincennes Railroad Company, with an authorized capital of $3,000,000. It was approved January 17, 1835. Charters were granted in something like the following order :

An act to incorporate the Jacksonville and Meredosia Railroad Company, capital stock $100,000, with a clause permitting the directors to double the amount, also to build a lateral road to Naples, was approved by the Governor, Feb. 5, 1835.

An act to incorporate the Belleville and Mississippi Railroad Company, with an authorized capital of $200,000, was approved Dec. 28, 1835.

The Winchester, Lynnville and Jacksonville Railroad Company was chartered with an authorized capital of $300,000, Jan. 8, 1836.

An act to incorporate the Pekin and Tremont Railroad Company, with an authorized capital of $150,000, was approved Jan. 13, 1836.

The Warsaw, Peoria and Wabash Railroad Company, with a capital of $150,000, was chartered Jan. 14, 1836.

The Wabash and Mississippi Railroad Company, with an authorized capital of $3,000,000, and the privilege of increasing the amount to $5,000,000, was chartered Jan. 15, 1836.

Separate bills, incorporating eight railroad companies, under the following titles, were approved Jan. 16, 1836 :

1. Pekin, Bloomington and Wabash Railroad Company. Capital, $500,000.

2. Mississippi, Springfield and Carrolton Railroad Company. Capital, $800,000, with authority to increase it indefinitely.

3. Alton, Wabash and Erie Railroad Company. Capital, $2,000,000.

4. Central Wabash Railroad Company. Capital, $50,000.

5. Galena and Chicago Union Railroad Company. Capital, $100,000.

6. Mount Carmel and Alton Railroad Company. Capital, $1,000,000.

7. Waverly and Grand Prairie Railroad Company. Capital, $500,000.

8. Rushville Railroad Company. Capital, $150,000.

After a respite of two days, bills were passed and approved, on the 18th of the month, chartering four more companies:

1. The Alton and Shawneetown Railroad Company. Capital, $500,000, with authority to increase it to $1,500,000.

2. The Shawneetown and Alton Railroad Company. Capital, $1,000,000, with authority to increase indefinitely.

3. Wabash and Mississippi Railroad Company. Capital, $400,000.

4. Illinois Central Railroad Company. Capital, $2,500,000.

I presume the object in granting charters to two companies between Alton and Shawneetown was, that one might begin at each end and work until they met, similar to the Central Pacific and Union Pacific.

The Caledonia Railroad Company, with an authorized capital of $300,000, was chartered Jan. 21, 1836.

Each and every company were authorized to lay either single or double tracks, and to propel their cars by steam, animals or any mechanical power. On some of the roads the rate of toll was fixed, and provisions made for all persons to run their own vehicles, under regulations similar to those for boating on canals.

CANALS.

Canals received the attention of the law-makers also. An act was passed and approved Feb. 10, 1835, authorizing the State to construct the Illinois and Michigan Canal, in which the Governor was authorized and directed to negotiate a loan of $500,000, to commence the work.

January 9, 1836, the foregoing law was repealed, and with some alterations was re-enacted. That, with the amendments subsequently added, was the authority under which the canal was built.

About this time laws were enacted for building half a dozen other canals, but no work was ever done on them.

INTERNAL IMPROVEMENT ACT.

The railroad laws of 1835 and '36 were never of more value than so much waste paper, for there was never a mile of road built under their authority; but from subsequent events it would appear that the people were only practicing in order to learn how to make laws. The most remarkable act ever passed by a legislative body in the State, was approved Feb. 27, 1837. It was entitled "An act to establish and maintain a general system of internal improvements." Two supplementary acts were approved March 4, 1837. The three acts are comprised in sixty-three sections, and fill thirty-two octavo pages. The object was to construct public improvements, in all parts of the State, at the expense of the State. A board of three Fund Commissioners was created, to manage the finances; also, a Board of Public Works, consisting of seven commissioners. The latter board was authorized to employ engineers, who were to lay out and superintend all public works. The board was authorized and required to adopt such measures as might be necessary to construct and complete within a reasonable length of time the following works. The amount of money named in connection with each one, was appropriated from the State treasury to defray the expense:

1. The improvement of the navigation of the Great Wabash River, $100,000; provided a similar amount was expended for the same purpose, by the State of Indiana.
2. The improvement of the navigation of the Illinois River, $100,000.
3. The improvement of the navigation of Rock River, $100,000.
4. The improvement of the navigation of the Kaskaskia River, $50,000.
5. The improvement of the navigation of the Little Wabash River, $50,000.
6. For the Western Mail Route, from Vincennes to Saint Louis, $250,000.

RAILROADS AGAIN.

7. A railroad from Cairo to some point near the southern termination of the Illinois and Michigan Canal, thence to Galena, $3,500,000.
8. A Southern Cross Railroad, from Alton to Mount Carmel; also a railroad from Alton to Shawneetown, $1,600,000.
9. A Northern Cross Railroad from Quincy, on the Missisippi river, to the Indiana State line, by the way of Mount Sterling, Meredosia, Jacksonville, Springfield, Decatur and Danville, thence to the State line, in the direction of Lafayette, Indiana, $1,800,000.

5—

10. A branch of the Central Railroad from Hillsboro, by the way of Shelbyville, in the direction of Terre Haute, Indiana, $650,000. Provision was made for the Alton, Wabash and Erie road, chartered the year before, to connect with this road.

11. A railroad from Peoria to Warsaw, on the Mississippi river, by the way of Canton, Macomb and Carthage, $700,000.

12. A railroad from Lower Alton, via Upper Alton and Hillsboro, to the Central Railroad, $600,000.

13. A railroad from Belleville, via Lebanon, to intersect the railroad from Alton to Mount Carmel, at the nearest eligible point, $150,000.

14. A railroad from Bloomington to Mackinaw town, there to fork, one line to touch the Illinois river at Pekin, the other at Peoria, $350,000.

15. In order to reconcile the representatives from those counties, that were not touched by any of the works included in this system, an appropriation was made to be equally divided among those counties according to population. The money was to be expended in building bridges, constructing roads and other improvements, $200,000.

Provision was made in the law for work to begin at both ends of all important roads, and at all the large towns; and to commence at both sides of all large streams that were crossed, and work both ways. This was done to keep all parties in the "ring" satisfied.

The Fund Commissioners were instructed to negotiate loans, to the amount of $8,000,000, for which they were to issue Certificates of Internal Improvement stock.

PRIVATE RAILROAD LAWS OF 1837.

After looking at the work laid out, to be done under the internal improvement laws, and the appropriation of money from the public treasury, to satisfy those who were living in counties not provided for, it seems incredible that at the same session there should have been parties who were still so anxious for railroad laws, that they besieged the legislature for private acts on the subject. The following are the titles under which some of the charters were granted:

Jacksonville and Naples Railroad Company, with authorized capital stock of $200,000; approved Feb. 18, 1837.

Canton and Utica Railroad Company, capital stock, $50,000, with authority to increase to $100,000; approved Feb. 24, 1837.

Mississippi and Illinois Railroad Company, capital stock, $700,000; approved Feb. 24, 1837.

Carrolton and Bluffton Railroad Company, with an authorized capital of $150,000, and permission to increase it to $200,000; approved Feb. 27, 1837.

Shohokon and Rushville Railroad Company, capital, $200,000, with privilege to increase indefinitely; approved Feb. 28, 1837.

The Danville and Covington Railroad Company, capital $100,000; was approved March 1, 1837.

Liverpool, Canton and Knoxville Railroad Company; was approved March 1, 1837.

Edwardsville and Chippewa Railroad Company, capital $50,000, with privilege of increasing to $100,000; was approved March 1, 1837.

Pittsfield and Mississippi Railroad Company, capital $600,000; was approved March 1, 1837.

Liberty and Pinckneyville Railroad Company, capital $150,000; was approved March 1, 1837.

Kaskaskia Railroad Company, capital 500 shares; was approved March 1, 1837.

Lewiston and Liverpool Railroad Company, capital $300,000; was approved March 2, 1837.

Manchester and Bridgeport Railroad Company, capital $100,000; was approved March 2, 1837.

Canton and Piketon Railroad Company, capital $250,000; approved March 3, 1837; re-chartered Feb. 26, 1839.

Jonesboro and Mississippi Railroad Company, capital $50,000; approved March 3, 1837.

Galena Railroad Company, capital $500,000, with authority to increase it to $1,000,000; approved March 3, 1837.

Tamaroa and Mississippi Railroad Company, capital $200,000; was approved March 3, 1837.

Wabash and Indiana Railroad Company, capital $1,000,000; was approved March 4, 1837.

Chester, Nashville and Pinckneyville Railroad Company, capital $300,000; was approved March 4, 1837.

Springfield and Beardstown Railroad Company, capital $200,000; was approved March 4, 1837.

Webster, Ottawa and Kishwakee Railroad Company, capital $500,000, with authority to increase it to $1,000,000; was approved March 4, 1837.

Chicago and Michigan Railroad Company, capital $1,000,000.

NET RESULTS OF TWO YEARS' LEGISLATION.

Western farmers are accustomed to such enormous crops that they soon become careless, and leave as much in harvesting, sometimes, as would be thought a fair crop in other parts of the country. In collecting the information with reference to the early legislation in Illinois for railroads and other internal improvements, I have endeavored to be more careful than the farmers; but where legislative bodies have yielded such luxuriant crops, I may have overlooked some of the laws. The net result, so far as my investigation goes, is something like the following:

The capital authorized to joint stock companies by the Legislature of Illinois, from January 17, 1835, to February 27, 1837, was $12,450,000, chiefly to railroad companies.

The internal improvement act of February 27, 1837, appropriated $10,200,000 directly from the State treasury. More than nine millions of this sum was for railroads.

At the same session private laws were enacted, chartering joint stock companies with authorized capital stock, to the amount of nearly $8,000,000, making an aggregate of about $30,000,000, involved in efforts to legislate railroads into existence in the State of Illinois before their time. The $20,000,000 of authorized stock to corporations, resulted in but little loss to the State or the people, as few of the companies ever organized, and those that did generally fell still born. The greatest loss from this source was the useless mass of legislation.

This gigantic system of internal improvements was inaugurated when the county was but sparsely settled, and before it was in a condition to export anything that would command money. The people imagined themselves rich, because the whole United States, east, west, north and south, was flooded with irredeemable paper money. It was thought there would be no difficulty in negotiating loans to carry forward the public works.

It has been suggested that the only reason why the General Assembly of Illinois did not, at that time, build an Insane Asylum, and resolve that its members should become inmates of it, was because it was not believed there were enough sane men belonging to their honorable body to run the new institution.

Soon after the law was enacted, certificates of internal improvement stock were readily taken, contracts let, and work commenced at various points, in all parts of the State. Millions of dollars were squandered in this way before the autumn of 1837, when the great financial crash, which commenced in the eastern cities, swept over the whole United States, and the internal improvement system of Illinois went down, leaving the State in what was thought, at the time, to be hopeless bankruptcy.

FIRST LOCOMOTIVE IN ILLINOIS.

Among the first lines upon which work was commenced under the internal improvement system, was the Northern Cross Railroad. The first ground was broken between Jacksonville and Meredosia, on what was called Wolf Run. It was about six miles east of the Illinois River. This was early in the spring of 1837. James Dunlap, now of Jacksonville, and T. T. January, of St. Louis, were the contractors. In the spring of 1838 the first locomotive engine ever brought to the State came up the Illinois River on a steamboat, and was landed at Meredosia. It was used for running construction trains from that time forward. This engine was built by Rogers, Ketchum and Grosvenor, of Patterson, New Jersey, and was called the "Superior." The road was so far advanced that the locomotive run into Jacksonville in the latter part of 1838 or early in 1839.

The work on the Northern Cross Railroad struggled along, after the internal improvement system had ceased in nearly every other part of the State. After it was put in running order from Meredosia to Jacksonville, some work was done between the latter place and Springfield, but for a year or two it moved slowly. In some way the canal fund became indebted to the internal improvement fund. On the 26th day of February, 1841, an act of the General Assembly was approved, providing for the completion of the Northern Cross Railroad from Springfield to Jacksonville. To liquidate the indebtedness of the canal fund to the internal improvement fund, $100,000 of canal bonds were appropriated to defray the expense of completing that part of the road. The Fund Commissioner was authorized and instructed to enter into contracts for the work, to be paid for with the canal bonds, and to be completed in one year. On the day following—February 27, 1841—a law was enacted requiring the Fund Commissioner to advertise for proposals to do the work. He was, by the same law, directed to take charge of all the work between Springfield and the Illinois River.

FIRST LOCOMOTIVE IN SPRINGFIELD.

Before the road was completed to Springfield, another locomotive was brought on, from the works of M. W. Baldwin, of Philadelphia. It was called the "Illinois." The track was so far completed that on the 15th of February, 1842, it entered Springfield, being the first one to arrive in the city. I had considerable difficulty to settle this point, but my authority is Mr. George Gregory, now a wealthy farmer, living about five miles west of the city, and Mr. T. M. Averitt whose home is on Jefferson street, near Eleventh. Mr. Gregory was the engineer, and Mr. Averitt the fireman. After conferring with each other they agree that it was in February, 1842—but Mr. Gregory is not sure of the exact day; Mr. Averitt remembers distinctly that it was the 15th. The track was laid along Tenth street to the crossing of Adams. The last half or three-fourths of a mile of the track was only the wooden stringers, the iron not yet having been spiked on. The newspapers were not very enterprising, with reference to the latest news, especially when we consider how wild they were on the subject of railroads only two or three years before.

Ten days after the event, February 25, I find in the *Sangamo Journal*: "The railroad is so far finished that the locomotive occasionally runs upon it, and has drawn at least one heavy load of produce to the river. Under the circumstances of the times, the contractors, Messrs. Duff, Calhoun & Co., have done well to complete it thus early. We anticipate that much business will be done on this road in the spring."

Again, from the *Journal* of March 11:

"NORTHERN CROSS RAILROAD. — We have neglected to notice that the railroad from this place to Meredosia, on the Illinois River, has been completed for a couple of weeks so far as to permit the passage of trains of cars through the whole line. The locomotive has now commenced trips between this city and the Illinois River; and, for the present, we understand it is arranged that the locomotive will leave this city every Monday, Wednesday and Friday, and Meredosia every Tuesday, Thursday and Saturday. We also learn that the steamer "Mungo Park" will run regularly between Meredosia and St. Louis, going and returning three times a week, so as to connect regularly with the train of cars. This arrangement will be of immense utility to our citizens and the traveling community, and will furnish the easy means of conveying to market the produce of a large and most productive region of country."

March 18, 1842, the *Journal* says: "On Saturday last, March 11, the cars ran from Jacksonville, 33½ miles, in two hours and eight minutes, including stoppages. It is believed the distance can be passed over in one hour and a half. Trips continue to be made three times per week."

March 25 we find in the *Journal*:

"PLEASURE TRIP.—On Monday, March 21, a large party left this city for Jacksonville, filling two passenger cars and another fitted up temporarily for the band of music. They speak in high terms of the hospitality and kindness of the citizens of Jacksonville, of the party there, and the pleasure of the trip."

In that paper, of the same date, we find: "During the few days the Springfield and Meredosia Railroad has been in operation, and before the public generally were aware of the running of the cars, the receipts from passengers alone have amounted to about seven hundred dollars."

This road was all made by laying long pieces of timber lengthwise with the track—cross pieces were placed six or eight feet apart, to keep the stringers from spreading—flat iron rails were spiked on to the pieces of timber, and then it was ready to receive the locomotive and cars.

After running awhile the engines needed repairing, and the track became uneven, so that the cars ceased to be run by steam. The road was then leased, and mule teams took the place of the locomotives. After becoming so dilapidated that it was a public nuisance, a law was enacted authorizing the sale of the entire road. The sale was effected for a mere trifle, with the stipulation that the parties coming in possession of it should put it in running order, for the accommodation of the public. This was something like the manner in which the internal improvement system of Illinois was closed out, after having started with $10,000,000, appropriated from the State treasury. There are men who assert that the disasters were all occasioned by a misnomer, that might have been avoided by erasing the letter *t* and inserting the letter *f*, in the first part of the name. Had that been done, the true character of the enterprise would have been understood and the danger averted. But Illinois has profited by instruction, obtained through disaster, and has, for many years, been marching with rapid strides on the true road to greatness.

After the Northern Cross Railroad passed out of the hands of the State, other changes followed, until it became a part of the

TOLEDO, WABASH AND WESTERN RAILWAY.

This road runs the entire distance across the State, from east to west, and touches all the principal points mentioned in the act incorporating the Northern Cross road.

The Toledo, Wabash and Western is one of the most important roads in the country—being the shortest route from the Atlantic seaboard to Northern Missouri and Kansas. The whole line, with its branches, comprises 814 miles.

	Miles.
The Main Line is	476
St. Louis Division (from Decatur to St. Louis)	106
Keokuk Branch	43
Hannibal Branch	50
Pekin Branch (from Decatur to Pekin)	65
Pittsfield Branch	6
Moberly Branch (in Missouri)	68
Total	814

Of these 814 miles there are in Illinois

	Miles.
Main Line	226
St. Louis Branch	106
Pekin Branch	65
Keokuk Branch	43
Hannibal Branch	50
Pittsfield Branch	6
Total in Illinois	496

The Illinois Division comprises all West of Danville, except the St. Louis Branch, which is a division by itself.

The Toledo, Wabash and Western is not only the oldest road in the State, but is a very important one to Springfield. The company has, for several years, kept repair shops here, and in 1869 erected new buildings for their rapidly increasing machine works, at a cost of about $75,000.

There are sixty-two locomotives belonging to the Illinois Division, and all are kept in repair at this place. Occasionally the repairs are such as to be about equal to building a new engine. The new stock carried at these shops averages about $40,000.

During the building season of 1870, the company erected in Springfield a very fine and substantial passenger depot, with accommodations for all the offices belonging to the Illinois Division. This building cost $36,000, and the freight depot $8,000. These, with the machine shops, make the total cost of buildings belonging to the company at this place about $120,000. There are about one hundred and eighty men employed in the shops, thirty track men, and about one hundred train men, including conductors, engineers and firemen, making over three hundred of the employees of the company who have their homes in Springfield. They, with their families, make between twelve and fifteen hundred of the population.

The monthly pay roll averages something more than $20,000 per month, or a total of $250,000 per annum. The passenger earnings at this station for 1870, were $80,000; freight $72,000, making the total receipts $152,000. This shows that the money paid out by the company in Springfield is about $100,000 above the receipts annually.

J. H. Fancher is the accountant at the machine shops, and T. G. Gorman, master mechanic.

Col. R. Andrews, Superintendent of the Illinois Division, resides in Springfield, and has his office in the new depot building.

Other officers and employees in the same building are: K. H. Wade, master of transportation; D. G. Moore, chief clerk; T. L. Dunn, resident engineer; A. M. Gregory, stock and fuel agent; E. H. Ives, ticket agent; E. Dresser and J. A. Patterson, train despatchers.

CHICAGO, ALTON AND ST. LOUIS RAILROAD.

All efforts to connect Springfield and Alton, by railroad, either by private charter or under the internal improvement laws, having been abandoned, a company was incorporated Feb. 27, 1847, and called the Alton and Sangamon Railroad Company. The charter was amended by an act of the General Assembly, Jan. 29, 1851. It was again amended so as to extend it to Bloomington, Feb. 11, 1851, with an additional amendment, Feb. 17, 1851.

By an act of the General Assembly, June 19, 1852, the name was changed to the Chicago and Mississippi Railroad Company. The work was then being prosecuted vigorously, and on the 9th of September, 1852, the first locomotive came through from Alton to Springfield.

From the Springfield *Journal* of Monday, Oct. 10, 1852, I learn that an entertainment was given in Springfield by the railroad company, to a party of excursionists from St. Louis and Alton. The steamboat Cornelia left St. Louis with the excursionists at six o'clock on the morning of Thursday, Oct. 6th, and arrived at Springfield at two o'clock, P. M., where a sumptuous dinner awaited them, in a building erected for a machine shop. The road was built chiefly through the exertions of the late Benjamin Godfrey, of Alton, who was introduced by the Hon. Virgil Hickox, now the General Agent of the road at this place. After a brief address from Mr. Godfrey, and speeches from some others of the party, and the dinner had been partaken of by all, the train moved away with its four hundred passengers on the return trip, and by nine o'clock that evening the excursionists were in their homes. This was an important event in the history of Springfield, as it opened direct communication with St. Louis and the South.

By an act of the Legislature, Feb. 11, 1853, the capital stock of the company was increased; and the charter amended Feb. 28, 1854.

On the 18th of October, 1853, the road was completed to Normal, forming a junction with the Illinois Central, by which passengers could go to LaSalle, and from there to Chicago by the Chicago and Rock Island road. This opened up the first communication by railroad from New York city to the Mississippi river. On the 4th of August, 1854, the present Chicago and Alton road was completed to Joliet.

Feb. 14, 1855, by an act of the General Assembly, the name of the company was changed to Chicago, Alton and St. Louis, and by the 21st of Jan., 1857, the company concluded to run the other way, and another act of the Legislature changed the name to St. Louis, Alton and Chicago Railroad Company.

Feb. 4, 1859, a charter was granted for the Alton and St. Louis Railroad Company. Previous to that time the communication between Alton and St. Louis was by steamers, on the Mississippi river. Feb. 19, 1859, the name was changed from St. Louis, Alton and Chicago to Alton, Chicago and St. Louis. Feb. 18, 1861, changed to Chicago and Alton.

After this, the Chicago and Alton and Alton and St. Louis roads were consolidated, forming the Chicago and St. Louis Railroad Company. Hon. Virgil Hickox, of this city, is the General Agent of the company.

From 1854 Springfield has had direct communication, by railroad, east, west, north and south, and by connections with other roads has had communication with all parts of the country. Nothing more was done for the city in the way of railroads until after the close of the great rebellion.

SPRINGFIELD AND ILLINOIS SOUTHEASTERN RAILWAY COMPANY.

A charter was granted for the Springfield and Pana Railroad Company, Feb. 16, 1857. The road was never built under that charter, but exactly eight years after, Feb. 16, 1865, another charter was granted, to cover the same ground and extend farther, under the title of the Pana, Springfield and Northwestern Railroad Company. Forty miles of this road —from Springfield to Pana—was completed and open for business in March, 1870. During the summer of 1870 it was put under contract to Beardstown, with the intention of extending it to Keokuk, Iowa. The work on this part of the road is completed, and the cars running to Virginia, in Cass county — thirty-two miles northwest of Springfield.

By an act of the General Assembly, approved March 5, 1867, a charter was granted for the Illinois and Southeastern Railway Company. This extends southeast from Pana to Edgewood, and includes the road already in running order from Edgewood to Shawneetown. The short link between Pana and Edgewood will be completed during the present season; then the line of road in running order will be two hundred and twenty-five miles long, from Shawneetown, on the Ohio, to Beardstown, on the Illinois River.

This line of road opens up to Springfield the finest body of timber land in the Western States. Forty miles of it, in the southeastern part of the State, runs through a dense forest of several species of the oak, hickory, sweet gum, black walnut, and other varieties of timber suitable for the manufacture of agricultural implements,cabinet furniture,etc.

An idea of its importance to Springfield may be formed, from the fact that the Springfield and Illinois Southeastern Railway Company have contracts already for supplying plow manufacturers in Moline with timber from these forests.

The officers of the company are : Thos. S. Ridgway, of Shawneetown, President; Charles A. Beecher, of Fairfield, Vice-President; George N. Black, of Springfield, Secretary; E. C. Dawes, Treasurer; Orland Smith, of Springfield, General Superintendent; Geo. W. Norris, Superintendent Southern Division; John Foggitt, General Freight Agent; Louis B. Smith, Auditor. Springfield is the headquarters of the company.

THE GILMAN, CLINTON AND SPRINGFIELD RAILROAD COMPANY

Was incorporated by an act of the General Assembly, March 4, 1867. An organization was effected at Clinton, April 21, 1869. Grading was commenced near Clinton, July 4th, 1870, and from that time until the close of the working season, from fifteen to eighteen hundred men were employed along the line. Track laying was commenced at Gilman, Feb. 19, 1871, and it is expected that the entire line, 110 miles in length, will be completed and running by the 4th of July. This will open up some of the finest agricultural country in the State—which has not heretofore been reached by railroads--and furnish a new route to Chicago, almost or quite as short as that by the Chicago and St. Louis railroad.

The principal office of this company is at Springfield, and the officers are: S. H. Melvin, of Springfield, President; William Fuller, of Clinton, Vice-President; John Warner, of Clinton, Treasurer; and Henry Crosley, of Clinton, Secretary.

SPRINGFIELD AND ST. LOUIS RAILROAD COMPANY

Was organized under the general railroad law of the State, August 4, 1870, with a capital stock of $800,000.

The object of this organization is to secure to Springfield a competing line to St. Louis, and also to furnish another through route from St. Louis to Chicago via Gilman. It runs almost in a straight line from Springfield to Litchfield, Montgomery county, thence to St. Louis. Its entire route is east of and eight miles shorter from Springfield to St. Loui sthan by the route of the Chicago, Alton and St. Louis road. This road will be put under contract this summer, and will, no doubt, be completed during the present year. The officers of the company are : S. H. Melvin, of Springfield, President; Robert McWilliams, of Litchfield, Vice President; George N. Black, of Springfield, Treasurer; P. B. Updike, of Litchfield, Secretary.

THE SPRINGFIELD AND NORTHWESTERN RAILROAD COMPANY

Was incorporated in 1869. It is to connect Springfield and Rock Island, by the way of Galesburg. Sept. 15, 1870, fifty miles—from Springfield to Lewiston—was put under contract, to be graded, ironed and furnished with rolling stock. It will be completed from Havana to Petersburg by the 1st of July, and from Petersburg to Springfield by the close of 1871.

The officers of the company are: W. C. Green, of Tallula, President; L. W. Ross, of Lewiston, Vice-President; John Williams, of Springfield, Treasurer; and Edward Lanning, of Petersburg, Sec'y.

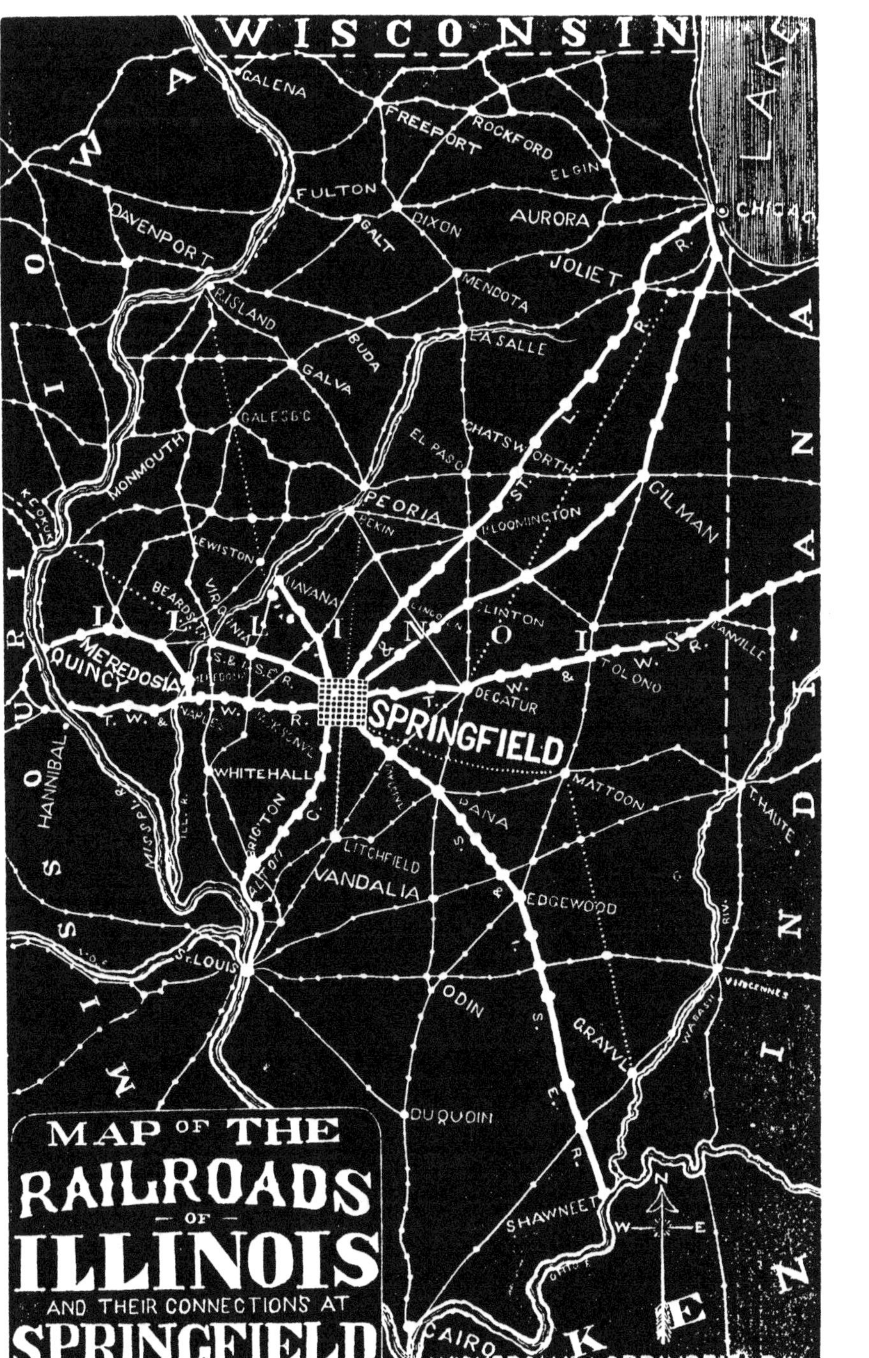
WISCONSIN
LAKE
IOWA
MISSOURI
ILLINOIS
INDIANA
KENTUCKY
GALENA
FREEPORT
ROCKFORD
ELGIN
FULTON
DIXON
AURORA
CHICAGO
GALT
DAVENPORT
JOLIET
MENDOTA
R. ISLAND
LA SALLE
BUDA
GALVA
GALESB'G
MONMOUTH
EL PASO
CHATSWORTH
PEORIA
PEKIN
BLOOMINGTON
GILMAN
LEWISTON
HAVANA
BEARDSTN
VIRGINIA
LINCOLN
CLINTON
DANVILLE
MEREDOSIA
QUINCY
TOLONO
DECATUR
SPRINGFIELD
HANNIBAL
WHITEHALL
MATTOON
PANA
T. HAUTE
LITCHFIELD
VANDALIA
EDGEWOOD
ST. LOUIS
VINCENNES
ODIN
WABASH
GRAYVL
DUQUOIN
SHAWNEET
CAIRO
N
W
E
MAP OF THE RAILROADS OF ILLINOIS AND THEIR CONNECTIONS AT SPRINGFIELD
WICKERSHAM-SPRINGFIELD.ILL.

THE SPRINGFIELD AND MATTOON RAILROAD COMPANY

Has $280,000 in subscriptions, voted by counties and townships, under the old constitution of the State. This line is seventy miles long, and is an extension of the Grayville and Mattoon Railroad. Operations are to commence on this line within a few weeks. The officers of the company are the same as those of the Grayville and Mattoon Railroad Company.

THE SPRINGFIELD AND PEORIA RAILROAD COMPANY

Was organized under the general laws of the State, August 16, 1870, and a board of directors chosen. The directors are: John T. Stuart, John Williams, J. C. Conkling and George N. Black, of Springfield; Milam Alkire, of Menard county; James Haines and Thomas King, of Pekin; and A. J. Hodges and Sidney Pulsifer, of Peoria.

SUBSCRIPTIONS.

Sangamon county, the city of Springfield, and the several townships named, have taken the following subscriptions by vote of the people:

The county has $100,000 in the Gilman, Clinton and Springfield road; and $100,000 in the Springfield and Illinois Southeastern road.

Springfield township has $80,000 in the Springfield and Illinois Southeastern; fifty thousand of it at one subscription, and thirty thousand at another.

Springfield towhship has $50,000 in the Springfield and Northwestern Railroad.

Salisbury township has $10,000 in the Springfield and Northwestern Railroad.

Woodside township has $20,000 in the Springfield and St. Louis Railroad.

HINT TO RAILROAD MEN.

By way of a hint to railroad men and capitalists, I would just ask them to look at the map, and see if there is not a splendid opportunity for a paying investment, in another Illinois Central Railroad. Commence at Cairo, and run via DuQuoin, or on a straight line west of that place, to Litchfield, Springfield, Pekin, Peoria and Freeport, thence to Madison, Wisconsin.

CONCLUSION.

It will be seen by the foregoing statements and consulting the map, that Springfield has six lines of railroads finished and running; two others upon which the work is far advanced, and will be completed within 1871; and three other organized companies, with such provision made as will secure the building of the respective roads. She will have at the close of this year eight, and at the end of two years, eleven roads; or as it were, spokes to a wheel, concentrating to and diverging from this point.

There are about fifty thousand miles of railroad in the United States. Of these Illinois has about one eighth, or something more than six thousand miles. It is with feelings of pleasure that I point to the map, engraved by a self-taught artist of Springfield, M. M. Wickersham, as a graphic description of the position the Capital of Illinois sustains to the general railroad system.

STREET RAILWAYS.

THE CAPITAL RAILWAY COMPANY

Was organized under the general laws of the State of Illinois, August 10, 1865, and permission was at once given by the City Council of Springfield, to locate the road on all the streets the company desired to occupy. They commenced operations with a capital of $18,000, which was afterwards increased to 28,000. The first board of directors were: J. K. Dubois, John Williams, D. L. Phillips, Alexander Starne and J. S. Bradford.

The officers chosen were: D. L. Phillips, President; John Williams, Treasurer; A. W. French, Secretary; Alexander Starne, Superintendent. John Williams afterwards resigned as Treasurer, and Jesse K. Dubois was chosen to fill the vacancy.

The road was built in the autumn of 1865, commencing at the old depot of the Toledo, Wabash & Western Railway, on the corner of Tenth and Monroe streets, and running west on Monroe street to Lincoln Avenue, one-third of a mile west of the city limits. It was opened for business January 1, 1866; the total cost to that time, being about $27,000.

The track was afterwards extended about one-third of a mile further west, and more recently about the same distance was taken up at the east end of the road—from Tenth to Seventh streets.

By an act of the General Assembly of Illinois, approved Feb. 25, 1867, the former transactions of the Capital Railway Company of Springfield, were legalized and its future rights and privileges defined. Its capital stock was fixed at $50,000, with authority to increase it indefinitely.

This road, running as it does, by the Post Office, and extending into the western part of the city, where the residences are numerous and increasing, is a great convenience. The Skating Rink is in that part of the city and is a place of great resort during the winter season.

The Capital Railway Company has a fine park or natural grove of eight or ten acres, at the western end of the road It is a fine place for picnics in the spring and summer season. No stranger visiting the city, should leave it until he has taken a ride to the west end of this line.

SPRINGFIELD CITY RAILWAY COMPANY

Was chartered Feb. 16, 1861, by a special act of the Legislature of Illinois, entitled "An act to promote the construction of Horse Railways in the city of Springfield." Jacob Bunn, John T. Stuart, Stephen T. Logan, Benjamin S. Edwards, Christopher C. Brown, Thomas S. Mather, and George Carpenter, were named as the first board of directors.

They were authorized to organize a company under the name that heads this article, with a capital stock of $50,000, and permission to increase it indefinitely. The company was invested with authority to build and operate street railroads, on any street in the present or future limits of the city, and to extend them to any point in the county of Sangamon. They were to go on any public highway, but were forbidden to put any obstruction in the way of travel.

This very liberal charter was not an exclusive one, but left the question so that other companies might avail themselves of the same privileges; therefore we find the Capital Railway Company, organized four and a half years later, with its road in operation before this one commenced work.

March 3, 1866, the Springfield City Railway Company was organized, by the election of the Hon. John T. Stuart, President; Asa Eastman, Vice President; George N. Black, Treasurer; and George Carpenter, Secretary. They commenced building the road at once and opened it for business on the 4th of July.

The original road commenced at Monroe street and ran north, on Fifth street to Oak Ridge Cemetery. The road, cars, and all the equipments cost $42,000. In the spring of 1867 it was extended on Fifth street to South Grand Avenue, at a cost of $13,000, making the total cost $55,000. The southern extension was opened for business just one year from the first opening, namely, July 4, 1867.

This company owns a fine park of twelve acres adjoining Oak Ridge Cemetery on the east. The park is finely shaded with native trees. It has a bountiful supply of pure well water, and a pagoda for refreshments. There is a stand on the ground fitted up for public speaking, with rustic bridges in appropriate places, and seats under almost every tree. These attractions, with a green turf over all the ground, make it a great resort for picnics.

This park and the fine walks and drives, among the sylvan groves of Oak Ridge Cemetery, forms a delightful retreat from the scorching heat and dusty streets of the city, in the summer months; and at all seasons, with the memories that cluster around the Lincoln Monument, it is one of the most attractive spots in the West, both to citizens and strangers.

The board of directors of the company are Jacob Bunn, John T. Stuart, J. W. Bunn, George N. Black, Asa Eastman, Dwight Brown, and C. W. Matheny.

The officers are Hon. John T. Stuart, President; Asa Eastman, Vice President; George N. Black, Treasurer; John W. Bunn, Secretary.

Mr. A. L. Ide was a director in the company until the last election, when he declined to serve longer in that capacity. He became Superintendent of the road about three months after it went into operation, and has continued in that position to the present time to the mutual satisfaction of the stockholders, and the people for whose convenience the road was built.

TOPOGRAPHY OF ILLINOIS AND STATISTICS OF POPULATION.

A brief statement will assist persons who have never been in this prairie country, to form some idea of its topography. Low water in the Ohio river at Cairo is 290 feet above the ocean's level. The water in Lake Michigan is 295 higher, or 585 feet above the ocean. The following table shows that Springfield is 48 feet higher than the lake, or 633 feet above the ocean's level. The average level of the State is probably from 650 to 700 feet above the ocean.

"The country is quite broken in the lead regions, and the hills are higher than in any other portion of the State, reaching an altitude, between Freeport and Galena, where the elevations are locally known as the *Mounds*, of from eight hundred and fifty to nine hundred feet above the level of the river at Cairo; and from five hundred and twenty-five to five hundred and seventy-five feet above the level of Lake Michigan; and from eleven hundred to eleven hundred and fifty above the ocean's level; and from two hundred to two hundred and fifty feet above the surrounding country."

Take the map and follow the line of the Chicago and St. Louis railroad. Joliet is in the valley of the Desplaines river; Wilmington at the crossing of the Kankakee; Pontiac at the crossing of the Vermillion, and Alton is a descent from the table land, to the margin of the Mississippi river.

The table lands between those rivers are the highest points. South and west from Chicago the country rises from 150 to 300 feet within the first hundred miles. Notwithstanding this, almost everybody says they are going *up* to Chicago; probably because it is very proper for a man to consider himself *gone up* when he arrives there.

Starting from Chicago, the column of figures on the left represents the number of feet the railroad track lies above or below the waters of Lake Michigan; those on the right the number of miles from that city:

		FEET.	MILES.
Joliet,	below	41	38
Elwood,	above	78	46
Wilmington,	below	21	53
Braidwood,	above	23	58
Braceville,	"	21	61
Gardner,	"	23	65
Dwight,	"	71	74
Odell,	"	144	82
Cayuga,	"	121	87
Pontiac,	"	86	92
Ocoya,	"	109	97
Chenoa,	"	153	103
Lexington,	"	196	111
TOWANDA,	"	228	119
Bloomington (Western station)		223	126
Shirley,	above	188	133
Funk's Grove,	"	148	137
McLean,	"	148	141
Atlanta,	"	162	147
Lawn Dale,	"	43	150
Lincoln,	"	31	157
Broadwell,	"	29	164
Elkhart,	"	35	168
Williamsville,	"	45	174
Sherman,	"	27	178
SPRINGFIELD,	"	48	185
Chatham,	"	60	194
Auburn,	"	84	200
Virden,	"	109	206
Girard,	"	111	210
Carlinville,	"	78	223
Shipman,	"	80	238
Brighton,	"	112	245
Monticello,	"	53	251
Alton,	below	112	257
St. Louis,	"	—	280

POPULATION OF STATE.

1810	12,282
1820	55,211
1830	157,445
1840	476,183
1850	851,470
1860	1,701,740
1870	2,529,410

POPULATION OF SANGAMON COUNTY.

1840	14,716
1850	19,228
1860	32,252
1870	46,384

POPULATION OF SPRINGFIELD.

1840	*1,600
1850	4,533
1860	9,320
1870	17,370

* Not official; all others taken from the United States census.

GEOLOGY OF ILLINOIS.

Very early in the history of the country, comprised at present in the State of Illinois, lead was discovered in the northwestern portion of the same, in what is now Jo Daviess county. The centre of this lead region is a little northeast of the city of Galena. Nearly all the lead produced by those mines, has been taken out within a radius of eight miles in diameter, around this central point. The lead bearing territory extends into Wisconsin and across into Iowa, but in northwestern Illinois it is confined to Stephenson and Jo Daviess counties.

Mining was prosecuted there previous to 1824, and attained its greatest importance about 1845, after which it declined. In 1853 the yield was 15,700 tons of 2,400 pounds each, which declined to 13,366 tons in 1858, and 8,262 tons in 1859. Mining is prosecuted there at the present time to a greater or less extent.

Lead is found in Hardin county, on the Ohio river, about three hundred and fifty miles south of the mines above described. The discovery was made by digging a well during the year 1839. No attention was given to it until 1841, when it was found in digging another well. In 1842 mining and smelting was commenced, but after sinking a great many shafts, the work was abandoned in 1851. It was not resumed until the autumn of 1865, when one of the old shafts was cleaned out ready for business. For the year ending December 1, 1867, one hundred and seventy-six thousand, three hundred and eighty-seven pounds of lead had been taken out. The number of laborers had increased from six to about sixty.

A story is related by Governor Ford, in his history of Illinois, connected with the early lead mining in this region of country. The business had been prosecuted for many years in Missouri, before it was discovered in the vicinity of what is now Galena. In 1824 the great richness of the Galena mines became known, and in the summers of 1825–6–7, hundreds and thousands of men from the southern part of Illinois would go up the Mississippi river on steamboats, in the spring, work in the lead mines through the warm weather, and return to their homes in the autumn, thus establishing a similarity between their migratory habits and that species of the finny tribe called Suckers. For this reason the Illinois miners were very early called "Suckers" by the few Missourians at Galena.

As the fame of these mines extended,

men from southern Missouri turned out in great numbers and flocked to Galena also. The circumstance of such numbers of unc outh men, coming up the river, was too suggestive to be lost. A facetious "Sucker" insisted that the Missouri lead mines had taken an emetic, and from that time the Missourians were called "Pukes." These appellations have been bandied back and forth in a good-natured way to the present time, and ludicrous incidents sometimes occur in the use of both.

SALT SPRINGS

Are found in several localities in the southern portions of the State. In the early settling of the country, when the transportation of merchandize was difficult, they were of great importance, and works for evaporating the water were erected in Saline and Jackson counties, and perhaps at some other points. In consequence of the weakness of the brine and the imperfect apparatus for evaporating, the works have been abandoned, except at Equality, in Saline county, where a small quantity is made. Prof. Worthen thinks that with improved methods for evaporation, it might be profitable to manufacture salt in Jackson county at the present time.

IRON MINING.

Hardin is the only county in the State where iron has been mined and furnaces erected for smelting it from the ore. A furnace was built there in 1837, and another in 1848. Charcoal, made from the heavy forests along the Ohio river, was used for smelting, and the iron produced commanded the highest price in the market. The furnace established in 1848 was closed in 1857. The first one opened, after being in operation twenty-four years, was closed in 1861, soon after the breaking out of the rebellion.

COAL AND COAL MINING.

The other minerals in this State are so meagre in supply as to be deserving of but a bare mention; but when we speak of coal, to say that it is abundant, gives but a meagre idea of its extent. It is found cropping out of the bluffs, along the water courses, over a large extent of country, and was mined in a rude manner by the first settlers. It is but a few years since the first attempts were made at mining on scientific principles.

A law was enacted by the General Assembly of Illinois, in February, 1851, authorizing the Governor, Auditor and Treasurer of the State to employ a Geologist, with the view of making an entire survey of the State. Three thousand dollars per annum was appropriated for the purpose of defraying the expenses of the same. The appropriation was to continue until the work was completed, or its discontinuance ordered by the Legislature.

At the session of 1853, the annual appropriations were increased to $5,000, and an additional $500 per annum for making maps of the several counties of the State. The survey was commenced in 1852 by Dr. J. G. Norwood.

In 1858 Prof. A. H. Worthen, the present State Geologist, was commissioned by Governor Bissell to take charge of the work. Annual reports were made to the Governor, without any appropriations for their publication until 1865. The general knowledge on the subject was so limited, and the desire of men of small calibre to make political capital under the convenient plea of economy, that a bill passed both Houses of the General Assembly, at the session of 1861, to repeal all laws on the subject, and thus recklessly throw away all that had been accumulated. The interposition of the veto by Governor Yates wrested the work from the hands of the destroyers.

At the session of 1865 an appropriation was made for the publication of the reports of the State Geologist. Early in 1866 the first volume of 504 octavo pages, with numerous illustrations, was published, and the second volume of 470 pages appeared the same year.

February 28, 1867, an act of the General Assembly was approved by Governor Oglesby, providing for the publication of the third volume of the reports, which appeared in 1868. It contained 574 pages. When the first volume of reports were prepared for the press there had not been a coal shaft sunk in Sangamon county, and Prof. Worthen says: "No coal has given me more trouble and has left me more uncertain about its geological horizon, than the bank of the Sangamon River."

In the third volume of his reports, speaking of the stratum mined in Sangamon county, by the shafts sunk since his first report, he says: "The coal from this seam is of excellent quality, and at some localities, as at Howlett, in Sangamon county, the coal is remarkably free from sulphuret of iron. * * * It is a harder and heavier coal than that from the seam above it, and appears to be by far the most valuable coal yet discovered in this portion of the State."

In the same volume he says: "The product of our coal mines for the past year, 1867, according to the most reliable statistics we have been able to obtain, is fully 1,500,000 tons. There is, perhaps, no other area of equal extent in the United States where coal is so easily obtained, with a moderate expenditure of capital, as in the Illinois coal fields." The facilities for mining have so increased since 1867, by sinking so many additional shafts, that the product has, no doubt, been doubled since that time.

An act of the General Assembly, approved by Governor Palmer March 11, 1869, provides for the publication of the fourth volume and for completing the fifth. There has also been an appropriation for publishing the fifth volume—the manuscript for which was ready as early as September, 1870. The fourth volume appeared in January, 1871. The materials for the sixth volume are collected, and I am informed, by Prof. Worthen, that it will be ready for the press during the current year, and only awaits an appropriation for its publication. When the fifth and sixth volumes are published, the entire survey of the State, by counties, will be before the people.

The report on Sangamon county is not yet published, but will be in the fifth or sixth volume. It will show that all the workable coal beds in the State underlie Sangamon county.

The accompanying section of the coal measures in Fulton county, copied from page 93, Vol. 4, report of State Geologist, will illustrate Sangamon county also:

Section of the Coal Measures in Fulton County.

4 to 6 feet.	Thin bedded gray limestone.
15 to 20 feet.	Shales but partially exposed.
	Coal seam No. 7.
37 feet.	Shale and sandy limestone.
3 to 5 feet.	Argillaceous limestone and bituminous shale.
	Coal seam No. 6.
5 to 10 feet.	Fire clay and nodular limestone.
15 to 20 feet.	Sandstone and shale.
2 to 3 feet.	Black shales and nodules of limest.

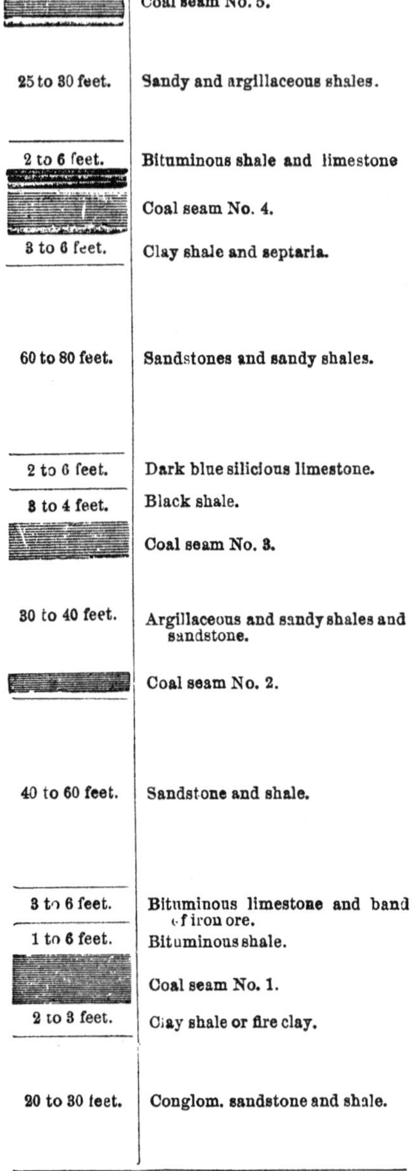

	Coal seam No. 5.
25 to 30 feet.	Sandy and argillaceous shales.
2 to 6 feet.	Bituminous shale and limestone
	Coal seam No. 4.
3 to 6 feet.	Clay shale and septaria.
60 to 80 feet.	Sandstones and sandy shales.
2 to 6 feet.	Dark blue silicious limestone.
3 to 4 feet.	Black shale.
	Coal seam No. 3.
30 to 40 feet.	Argillaceous and sandy shales and sandstone.
	Coal seam No. 2.
40 to 60 feet.	Sandstone and shale.
3 to 6 feet.	Bituminous limestone and band of iron ore.
1 to 6 feet.	Bituminous shale.
	Coal seam No. 1.
2 to 3 feet.	Clay shale or fire clay.
20 to 30 feet.	Conglom. sandstone and shale.

Prof. Worthen says: "The section constructed in this (Fulton) county will be considered a typical one, and will be used for the co-ordination of the coal strata throughout the central and western portion of the State. We have found, here, seven consecutive seams, all exposed by their natural outcrop, within the county, and all, except the upper one, have been worked to a greater or less extent. The aggregate thickness of these seams is about twenty-five feet, and their individual range is from twenty inches to six feet in thickness."

In a conversation with Prof. Worthen, which I am at liberty to use, he informed me that Sangamon county has all the workable coal strata found in any other part of the State; hence, there is at least twenty-five feet, in thickness, of coal underlying the county. The stratum penetrated by all the coal shafts in this county —of which I shall speak in another place —is either the fifth or fourth, he thinks it is the fourth.

The Illinois coal fields extend over three-fourths of the State. Coal is found in seventy-five of the one hundred and two counties of the State.

"The usual mining estimate for the productive capacity of a coal seam gives one million tons of coal to the square mile for every foot in thickness that the seam will measure."

In order to illustrate the inexhaustibleness of the supply, we will take ten miles square, of which Springfield is the centre. This makes one hundred square miles. The stratum now being worked is six feet thick. If one foot depth, over one square mile, gives one million tons, six feet depth gives six million tons. Multiply that by one hundred, and it gives six hundred millions of tons or fifteen thousand millions of bushels on ten miles square. And this stratum is only one-fourth of the aggregate thickness of the coal we have.

ARTESIAN WELL.

In the year 1857 an arrangement was made, by which the City Council of Springfield, and some of the public spirited citizens, agreed to contribute equally for the purpose of sinking an Artesian Well. June 15, 1857, an ordinance was passed, appropriating $3,000 to defray the expense on the part of the city. December 20, 1858, $2,000 more was appropriated, and again $2,000 March 7, 1859.

Ex-Mayor John W. Priest was then Mayor of the city. From him I learn that the last appropriation was never used. The whole amount expended was about $10,000—half by the city and half by subscribers. The boring was carried down about eleven hundred feet and then abandoned, leaving the greater part of the machinery in the earth. In passing through the stratum of coal now mined here, Prof. Norwood, the State Geologist, was in attendance, and pronounced the coal to be from twenty to twenty-four inches in thickness. The failure to understand its extent was, no doubt, owing to the fact that no precautions had been taken to keep out the water and mud from the boring. Mayor Priest says that if its real extent had been known, there is but little doubt that a shaft would have been sunk and mining commenced at that time. The boring was done at the side of Washington street, near the eastern limits of the city.

COAL MINING.

THE HOWLETT MINE.

The village of Howlett is seven miles east of Springfield, at the east side of Sangamon River, and is in this county. It was formerly called Jamestown. On the 18th of December, 1865, Mr. P. L. Howlett, who was then running a distillery at that place, attached boring apparatus to the machinery of his distillery, and commenced boring on the bank of the Sangamon, about twenty-five feet from the distillery. On the 4th of April, 1866, he reached the coal, at a depth of 210 feet. After passing through the coal, he supposed it to be eight feet thick. Many persons thought he was deceived in the thickness, among others Prof. Worthen, the State Geologist, who thought the signs of coal might have been occasioned by pieces falling from the thin veins passed through above. Not willing to risk the expense of sinking a shaft while there was any doubt with regard to the existence of coal, although he was convinced in his own mind, Mr. Howlett moved his machinery to a more suitable place for sinking a shaft, by the side of the Toledo, Wabash and Western Railroad, and commenced boring again May 4, 1866. This time he put down five inch iron tubing, in order to keep any pieces of coal from falling out of the veins that he might pass. At a depth of 197 feet he again reached what he supposed to be the coal, and, according to previous agreement, sent for Prof. Worthen, who remained until the drill passed through the coal, which he pronounced to be eight feet thick. It was afterwards ascertained that a little more than two feet of this was bituminous shale. June 5th he commenced sinking a shaft, and Sept 5th, 1867, reached the coal, and at once commenced mining it to supply the market. The following statement of the substances passed through will give some idea of the geology of this part of the country:

		FEET	INCHES
	Clay	11	0
	Soapstone	3	0
	Black Shale	2	9
7.	Coal	1	10
	Fire Clay	3	0
	Blue Limestone	3	0
	Light Marl	18	0
	Sand Stone	49	9
	Blue Soap Stone Shale	16	2
	Hard blue Fos. Rock with iron balls.	3	0
	Black Shale	0	1
6.	Coal	0	2
	Fire Clay	4	6
	Dark Blue Shale	3	10
	Reddish Gray Clay Shale	7	6
	Very hard Conglomerate Rock	3	6
	Reddish Gray Clay Shale	4	6
	Black Clay Shale	1	0
	Reddish Gray Clay Shale	4	6
	Gray Lime Rock	8	0
	Gray Shale	2	0
5.	Coal and Rock mixed	1	0
	Fire Clay	7	6
	Light Sand Rock	16	0
	Gray Shale	16	2
	Variegate Lime Rock	1	6
	Hard Black Shale	2	6
4.	Coal	5	10
	Fire Clay	3	0
		205	6

Soon after opening the mine, Mr. Howlett caused some of the coal to be sent to Chicago, to be analyzed by Prof. Blaney. After analyzing it, Prof. Blaney says:

"The following is the composition of the coal, analyzed at your request:

Moisture	6,480
Volatile combustible matter	36,765
Fixed carbon	48,203
Ash	8,552
	100,000

"No test was made of the percentage

of sulphur in the coal, as there was not enough for that purpose; but, from its appearance and the color of the ash, I am of the opinion that the amount must be very small.

"The large proportion of volatile combustible matter in this coal would indicate a peculiar fitness for the manufacture of gas, as it is in this respect superior, in percentage, to the Youghogheney coal, of Pennsylvania, which is considered to be the standard coal for the manufacture of gas."

After having his mine in good working order, Mr. Howlett loaded several cars with coal and shipped it to Carondelet, Missouri, to have it tested in making iron. The following from the foreman of the iron works and from the proprietors, will show the result :

CARONDELET, Mo., May 14, 1868.

This is to certify that I have managed the smelting of iron ore with coal brought here by P. L. Howlett, and it has far exceeded my expectation, making a good quality of iron, and more of it in twenty-four hours, than any other coal used in this—Carondelet—furnace; and I further say that I have been raised a furnace-man, and followed it all my life, and am now forty-eight years old; and I never have seen as soft, solid, white iron as this coal has made, and think that if I could have a fortnight's run on it I would be able to make A No. 1 foundry iron with it, as it always requires some time to adjust the proportions of iron ore, lime and other materials to bring about the desired change.

ROBERT ADAMS.

From the proprietors of the furnace:

ST. LOUIS, May 16, 1868.

P. L. Howlett, Esq., St. Louis Mo.

DEAR SIR : The test made of "Carondelet Furnace" pig iron shows a tensile strength of twenty-seven thousand (27,000) pounds. The test made of the same, from one of the first heats, stood 12,000. Brazil pig stood 6,000. The standard for C. B. (cold blast) charcoal, is 22,000 to 24,000. Our H. B. No. 1 charcoal is about 16,000. Respectfully,

M. WOODWARD, *Treas.*

The above test was made on iron made at our furnace, from Iron Mountain ore, and coal furnished by P. L. Howlett, from his mines near Springfield, Ill.

MCKERNAN, LILLY & CO.

Mr. Howlett continued to work the mine until September, 1869, when it went into the hands of Jacob Bunn, of Springfield. March 20, 1870, the shaft, with 720 acres of land, was leased to C. O. Godfrey, of Hannibal, Mo. In May, 1870, the Western Coal and Mining Company was organized at Springfield, under the general laws of Illinois, with a capital of $500,000. The Howlett mine then passed from the hands of C. O. Godfrey to the Western Coal and Mining Company. This mine is now in a condition to take out 250 tons of coal per day. It keeps about 75 miners employed in summer, and about 125 in winter, or an average of 100. The company has two mines at Danville, and have secured lands preparatory to opening one at Chapin, ten miles west of Jacksonville. They keep coal yards at Logansport, Lafayette, Decatur, Jacksonville and Springfield. At the Springfield yard there is always a supply of the Howlett coal. In addition to this they keep Blossburg and Anthracite coal and Connelsville coke, being the only yard in Springfield where such an assortment is to be found.

The officers of the Western Coal and Mining Company are C. O. Godfrey, President; Edward Price, Secretary; F. Wilms, Cashier; A. J. Bean, Superintendent. The principal office of the company is under the Leland Hotel, at Springfield.

J. G. LOOSE'S MINE—SOUTH SHAFT.

When Mr. Howlett commenced boring for coal, Mr. Loose was on the point of commencing also. He then made arrangements with Mr. Howlett to take his machinery, after that gentleman had gone as deep as he desired; but when Mr. Howlett decided to bore a second time, Mr. Loose sent to the oil regions of Pennsylvania, obtained a complete outfit and commenced boring in June, 1866.

He went down to the coal, satisfied himself, and commenced sinking a shaft in Sept.. He kept the work moving the entire winter, and in April, 1867, reached the coal. In a very short time he was ready to supply the market, being the first man in the county to take coal from a shaft.

His mine is 237 feet deep, and curbed with timber eight inches thick. It is caulked with oakum down to the first stone, seventy feet, in order to keep out the water. The shaft is eight by sixteen feet, and divided into three compartments—two of equal size, for the downward and upward movement of the cages, and a smaller one for ventilation. A furnace is built about seventy feet from the eye of the shaft, inside the mine, and is connected by a horizontal flue with the compartment for ventilation. A fire kept burning in the furnace, produces a vacuum in the mine, which causes a current of cold air to flow down the two main compartments in the shaft, and the heated air passes up through the ventilating compartment, thus keeping the air in the mine pure.

The money expended in sinking this shaft and fitting it up with steam engine, hoisting machinery and buildings, is about $80,000. Mr. Loose employs from fifty to one hundred miners, and takes out an average of about 200 tons per day. Being at the crossing of two railroads, he has his machinery so arranged that he can coal two engines, load two cars and three wagons, at once, and if all were ready at the same moment, it could be done in one minute of time.

SAUNDERSON & CO.'S MINE—NORTH SHAFT.

William Saunderson and William Beard, under the firm name of Saunderson & Beard, commenced Feb. 10, 1867, about one and a half miles north of the State House, and just outside of the city limits, at the east side of the Chicago and St. Louis Railroad, to sink a shaft. At a depth of sixteen feet they struck a vein of quicksand, which admitted so much water that they abandoned the spot and moved about three hundred yards further north and to the west side of the railroad.

Here they again commenced sinking a shaft, and after passing through several strata of coal too thin for mining, they came to a six foot stratum, at a depth of 248 feet. The shaft was completed July 15, 1867, but it was not until September that the buildings and machinery were ready for active operations. The works complete cost $40,000. In December, 1868, Charles Hickox was admitted a partner, and the style of the firm changed to Saunderson & Co.

During the winter months, about sixty miners are employed, but in summer the number is reduced about one-half. They take out of this shaft, on an average, the year round, about 100 tons, or ten car loads of coal per day, and have all the buildings, hoisting machinery and steam power, to take out 240 tons per day, if the market required it. Wm. Beard is is the Superintendent.

The works of this firm being at the side of a railroad track, and between the city and Sangamon river, are finely situated to attract manufactories around them. They are prepared to offer special inducements in the way of land grants, and the cheapest and best of fuel, to parties desiring to engage in any branch of manufacturing. Their facilities for natural drainage is unsurpassed, and their close proximity to the water works would make communication easy for any business that might require it. Manufacturers looking for a location should not fail to call on Messrs. Saunderson & Co.

STARNE & SHUTT'S MINE — WEST END SHAFT.

Hon. Alexander Starne and G. W. Shutt, Esq., under the firm name of Starne & Shutt, broke ground June 17, 1870, for the purpose of sinking a coal shaft. The site is at the north side of the northwestern extension, of the Pana and Southeastern Railroad, and is one and three-eighth miles west of the old State House. It is, therefore, very properly called the "West End Shaft."

From fifteen to twenty men were kept steadily at work, from the commencement until the 10th of September, when they reached a stratum of coal five feet ten inches thick, at a depth of 153 feet. The coal is the same as that mined in the other shafts in this vicinity, but the difference in depth is all on the surface. This mine commences in a valley where the surface is from seventy-five to one hundred feet lower than at the north or south shaft. The cost of sinking the shaft was about twenty thousand dollars, but the other improvements in the way of buildings for the mines and miners, grading and improving the grounds, has involved an outlay of nearly sixty thousand dollars.

This mine being yet new, has not room for a great number of miners to work, sixty-five being the most that has at any one time been engaged. They now keep thirty steadily at work, and take out from two to three thousand bushels, or from eighty to one hundred and twenty tons per day.

Their steam engine, hoisting apparatus, and all the other machinery and appliances are equal to either of the other shafts, and when business justifies, they could double the quantity of coal produced.

Messrs. Starne & Shutt have one hundred and ten acres of land connected with their coal shaft, and in addition to its value for mining has some splendid situations for manufacturing establishments. The facilities for natural drainage could not be better. Parties coming to Springfield for the purpose of seeking a location for almost any kind of a manufacturing establishment could not do better than by calling upon them.

WATER WORKS, SEWERAGE AND GAS.

SPRINGFIELD WATER WORKS.

For the purpose of establishing water works, the city authorities of Springfield, a few years ago, purchased thirty acres of land adjoining the city on the north. From the business part of the city to this land, the surface rises gently until an elevation of eleven feet above the old State House grounds is attained. For the purpose of commanding as great an elevation as possible, the surface was made the bottom of the reservoir, and an embankment of 100 feet wide at the base, sloping equally inside and out, until it was raised to 22 feet in height and 20 feet across the top. To make it water tight, the bottom and sides were puddled with blue clay and concrete, and the entire inside, except the bottom, covered with slabs of Joliet stone, imbedded in cement. One tier of slabs, or flag stones are laid flat on the top at the inner border, and a picket fence mounted on the stone around the enclosure.

The reservoir is a square, rounded at the corners. It is 200 feet in diameter at the bottom, and about 275 at the top, inside, and has a capacity of 4,000,000 gallons. The embankment is nicely sodded on the outside, and presents a beautiful appearance. The earth for making this embankment was taken from the grounds adjoining on the east, west and north, so as to make a miniature chain of lakes, with islands interspersed. These islands have shrubbery planted on them, and in time will form some of the most picturesque scenery imaginable. There is what is called a stand pipe in the centre of the reservoir. It stands on the bottom, and is seventy feet high. It is embedded in a pedestal of concrete masonry ten or twelve feet in diameter and octagonal in form. The pedestal rises four or five feet above the surface of the water. This stand pipe is made of iron, and is three feet or more in diameter. On the pedestal at each of the eight sides there is a sea horse rampant, and a huge dolphin, four of each alternating, the whole fronting outward. Just above this group, there is a vase, twelve or fifteen feet in diameter, and about ten feet above the vase, four swans, life size, attached to the stand pipe. Sea horses, dolphins, swans and vase, are all made of iron. The crest of the stand pipe is a combination of iron work, highly ornamental, and extending outward on all sides.

Three and one quarter miles north of the reservoir, on the bank of the Sangamon river, there is a house with a steam engine and two large pumps in it. There is also a very large well, about one hundred feet from shore, and connected by a tunnel. A very strong set of iron pipes, fifteen inches in diameter, is connected with the well and laid under ground; the three and a quarter miles to the reservoir passes under the embankment, and connects with the stand pipe at the bottom. These pumps at the river are so arranged that either one can be made to form the connecting link between the well and the pipe leading to the reservoir. When connected, one of them throws ordinarily 960 gallons per minute, 57,600 per hour, or 1,382,400 in twenty-four hours, and this quantity can be doubled in an emergency.

The top of the stand pipe is 170 feet higher than the pumps, and three and a quarter miles distant. Put the machinery in motion, and we can soon have the water issuing on all sides, in the form of spray, from the ornamental work at the top of the stand pipe, and falling over the swans into the vase; from there it is connected by pipes to the four dolphins below, and from the mouth of each of these a stream of water spouts into the reservoir. In order to conduct the water to where it is wanted for use, there is a fifteen inch pipe laid from the reservoir, under ground, about one mile into the city; and where it is necessary to branch off, ten inch pipe is used, and again four inch, and so on down to the small pipes, leading into the different rooms of the houses.

I have said that the ground on which the reservoir stands is eleven feet above the city, and the water in the reservoir twenty-two feet higher, making thirty-three feet it will rise—when the pipes are properly placed in the houses—on the principle that water will find its level. Some of the buildings are higher than this, and in order to supply them with water, the pumping machinery and pipes are so arranged, that when the engine is running at the river, water may be forced more than eighty feet above the surface, five miles away from the propelling power at the river.

These works are constructed with the view of supplying a city of forty or fifty thousand inhabitants, and as Springfield contains only about eighteen thousand, there is danger that too much water will be pumped up and overflow the reservoir. This, however, is guarded against by an opening in the stand pipe, a foot or more below the level of the embankments. This opening in the stand pipe is connected by a smaller pipe, passing down inside the stand pipe, and out under the embankments, to the artificial lake with the islands in it, around the reservoir, thus preventing an overflow and supplying the artificial lake by the same operation.

The whole work was designed by Mr. Henry Earnshaw, hydraulic engineer, of the Cincinnati water works. The engine, pumps, statuary, and all the ornamental iron work, was made at the foundry of Miles Greenwood, in Cincinnati. The construction of the work was superintended by John C. Ragland, of Springfield, under orders from the commissioners—John Williams, C. W. Matheney and Dr. H. Wohlgemuth. It was commenced June 1, 1866, and completed July 1, 1868, at a total cost of about $460,000.

In addition to supplying the dwellings, business houses, hotels, factories, etc., with water, fire plugs are placed at convenient distances from each other all over the city. With the two splendid steam fire engines, this affords ample protection against conflagrations; so that a fire very rarely extends beyond a building in which it originated.

All the additional expense necessary to supply a population of fifty thousand persons will be the additional supply pipes to convey the water where it is desired.

John C. Ragland continues to be the superintendent.

SEWERAGE OF THE CITY.

The southern one of the two ravines, between which the old North Carolina hunter pitched his tent, has for many years been called the Town Branch. It runs a little north of the Governor's Mansion, passes between the old and new State Houses, and running in a north-westerly direction, empties into Spring Creek, as already stated. Within the city limits it is all arched over and the ground leveled up above it. The opening is about ten feet in diameter, and is the main sewer for the drainage of the city.

The system of sewerage is very elaborate, having already between twenty-five and thirty miles completed, ranging in size from two to ten feet. The sewerage, like the water works, will require but a little extension of pipes, mostly smaller than those already laid, to bring it up to the necessities of an equally large population.

GAS LIGHT COMPANY.

Springfield Gas Light Company was chartered by the General Assembly of Illinois, Feb. 27, 1854, and was put in operation soon after. The works have been extended from time to time as the demand increased. The streets are lighted with gas, and large quantities of coke made, which is used in the foundries. Mr. N. H. Ridgley is the owner of nearly or quite all the stock.

CHURCHES.

BAPTIST.

First—Organized 1852. Number of members 340. Rev. Nehemiah Pierce, Pastor. Sabbath School has about 250 pupils. Geo. W. Ingalls, Superintendent.

North—Organized 1862. Number of members 160. D. F. Carnahan, Pastor. Sabbath School 120 scholars. D. F. Carnahan, Superintendent.

German—Organized 1864. Number of members 60. Rev. George Brentz, Pastor.

CATHOLIC.

Church of Immaculate Conception—Organized 1855. Number of members about 600 families or 3,000 persons. Rev. Father Brady, Pastor. Parochial Sabbath School contains 500 pupils, under the charge of the Sisters of Notre Dame, Mother Capstrana, and Patrick McMahan and Michael Kelly.

St. Peter's and St. Paul's—Organized 1865. Number of members 170 families or 700 persons. Rev. Father Lueken, Pastor. Sunday School numbers about 175 scholars, and is taught by Frederick Jasper and Michael Haider.

CHRISTIAN.

Organized 1838. Rev. J. B. Crane, Pastor. Number of members 250. Sabbath School contains 120 pupils. Wm. Lavely, Superintendent.

CONGREGATIONAL.

Organized February 6th, 1867, with 74 members. Rev. J. H. McLane, Pastor. Number of members 153. Sabbath School numbers 165 scholars. D. G. Moore, Superintendent. Cost of Church and furnishing about $12,000. Money raised in the last four years $25,000, in addition to $5,258, to pay off debt on Church lots. The Church has a standing offer of $1,500 towards a Church organ, which will be accepted, and the instrument procured.

PROTESTANT EPISCOPAL.

St. Paul's—Located at the corner of Third and Adams streets, is one of the oldest Churches or organizations in the city, having been established about the year 1836. Rev. Chas. Dresser, D.D., was the first Pastor, and served the Parish for seventeen years. The Rev. Jos. W. Pierson, Rev. L. P. Clover, Rev. W. F. B. Jackson, Rev. H. N. Pierce, D. D., and Rev. F. M. Gregg, A. M., have succeeded him. The Parish is now in a highly prosperous condition and fully organized for work, numbering more than one thousand, with two hundred families and about 250 communicants. The Sunday School numbers 325 scholars, with 65 officers and teachers. Hon. George H. Harlow is Superintendent. By a single effort this Church recently liquidated a debt of about $8,000.

HEBREW CONGREGATION,

Organized 1864. Rev. B. Deutsh, Pastor. Number of members 25. The Sabbath School numbers 12 members. Rev. B. Deutsh, Superintendent.

LUTHERAN.

English.—This Church was organized in the year 1841, by Rev. Francis Springer, a well-known divine and school teacher. The Church comprised eight members—Jacob Divelbiss and John B. Weber, Esqrs., being the only members thereof now in the city. The Church organization erected the present house of worship in the year 1853, at a cost of $8,000, since which time it has been considerably improved. The Pastor is Rev. E. E. Heilmann. Number of members 130. Sabbath School numbers 185 scholars. W. Fychon, Superintendent, and C. C. Cromwell, Assistant. In 1866 the Lutheran Church separated into two divisions, which produced a very disastrous result upon the workings and prosperity of the Church. It is hoped an union may soon be perfected, and the result thereof be highly beneficial to the organization.

METHODIST EPISCOPAL.

First.—Was organized in 1821, when there were about 40 members in this entire county; and was made a station in October, 1834, with 100 members, and legally organized in October, 1838. Rev. Franklin W. Phillips, Pastor. Sabbath School numbers 325 scholars, with 500 volumes in the library. A. W. Coleman, Superintendent.

Second.—Organized in 1865 with 75 members. Rev. E. D. Wilkin, Pastor. Number of members, 150. The Sabbath School numbers 150 scholars. R. F. Herndon, Superintendent.

German Methodist.—Organized in 1850, and church built in 1856. Rev. J. S. Keller, Pastor, Adam Donges, Local Preacher. Number of members, 34. Sabbath School has 60 scholars. Charles Kahn, Superintendent.

PRESBYTERIAN.

First.—Organized by Rev. John W. Ellis, January 30, 1828, since which time it has had five pastors. Rev. James A. Reed is the present pastor. The members of the congregation number 581, the communicants numbering 330. The Sabbath School contains 300 members. W. H. Hayden, Superintendent. Three colonies have been sent out by this church. In May, 1832, thirty members were dismissed to form the North Sangamon Church; in May, 1835, thirty were dismissed to form the Second Church of Springfield; and in January, 1849, forty-two were dismissed to form the Third Presbyterian Church.

Second.—Was organized May 26, 1835. Rev. Albert Hale, Pastor from July 1st, 1840, to January 1st, 1867. Rev. G. H. Robertson, the present Pastor, began his labors April 21st, 1867. The present number of members is 400. The Sabbath School numbers 325 scholars, and 35 teachers. George M. Brinkerhoff, Superintendent.

Third.—Organized February 7, 1849, with 44 members. A. Stone, James L. Lamb and E. R. Wiley, Elders. Rev. R. V. Dodge was installed the first Pastor, May 1, 1849, and resigned October 1, 1857. He was succeeded by Rev. J. C. Jennings, who in January, 1861, also resigned. Rev. G. W. F. Burch was installed October, 1861, and resigned September 31, 1867. Rev. H. L. Paynter is the present pastor; began his labors in June, 1870, and was installed October, 1870. The church is quite prosperous, and the week and Sabbath services well attended. The collections for the last year were nearly $3,000. The Sabbath School library contains 300 volumes. The Sabbath School numbers 200 scholars and 20 teachers. E. R. Uhlrich is Superintendent.

First Portuguese.—Organized ———. Pastor, Rev. H. L. Harvey. Number of members, 100. Sabbath School, 60 scholars.

Second. — Organized ———. Pastor, Rev. H. McKee. Number of members, 105. Sabbath School, 50 scholars.

UNIVERSALIST.

Organized by Rev. L. C. Marvin, Pastor, in 1852, and instituted in July, 1857. The society numbers 100 members, one-half of which number being members of the church. The church was dedicated December 24, 1858. Rev. Mr. Lombard, Pastor. The Sabbath School numbers 60 scholars, and H. F. Smith is Superintendent. Notwithstanding this church has had to contend against the most adverse circumstances and difficulties, it is now in a flourishing and prosperous condition.

CITY SCHOOLS.

By H. C. Watson.

In the list of advantages possessed by Springfield, none is greater than that of her institutions of learning, her temples of instruction and her seats of popular and general education. Conforming to the requirements of the age of progress and of advancement, readily appreciating and acknowledging the fact that a people, to be free, intelligent and useful, must be educated, our city government has sought, by extending a liberal hand, to foster and promote within our midst the glorious and beneficent scheme of popular education. Springfield has said unto her citizens, educate your children, instruct your youth, without money and without price—thus placing within the reach of all, even the lowest, humblest and poorest, the greatest blessing a government can bestow—a good and generous education.

In the earlier days of Springfield, ere her limits had been extended square miles, and her population was decidedly small, the educational facilities were not of the most magnificent description. No palatial school houses then reared their stately fronts within our limits, no school board supervised the movements of the educators of youth, and no army of teachers, patient, toiling instructors of the youthful mind were to be found within the boundaries of the city. These things belong to another day, are part and parcel of another system, another order and arrangement of affairs. "The boys of the period," in those days, obtained their supplies of "book larnin" —meagre and small as they were—from sources not so high or so grand, but far different indeed. One of the earliest, teachers who initiated those boys into the mysteries of reading and writing, and led them through the dark mysterious ways of arithmetic and grammar, was Beaumont Parks, Esq., (forever sanctified be his memory.) Plain and simple as the most artless boy under his direction, he was one of the best, most honest, and conscientious of teachers. Filled with a love of his profession, imbued with a strong desire to instruct the heart and mind of the youth committed to his control, that they might walk aright the pathway of life, he labored faithfully and diligently to discharge his duty. Possessed of a fine cultered mind, and of attainments decidedly rare in those days, he pursued his unostentatious calling, asking not for public praise or high sounding plaudits, but only for the satisfaction of knowing he had discharged his duties faithfully and well. Some of our most influential and prominent citizens were his pupils, and the powerful influence of his teachings have been exerted indeed for good. Only a few weeks ago and he was called hence, full of honors and of years: And although he lives not, his deeds remain.

Rev. Francis Springer, a gentleman of fine attainments and ability, was another pioneer in the cause of education. He taught as early as 1839. In 1847 the Southern Theological and Collegiate Institute was chartered and organized at Hillsboro, and he was elected President, which position he retained until 1855. In 1844 Mr. Springer assumed charge of the Springfield Academy, and continued until 1847. In August, 1856, he was elected Principal of the First Ward School, and elected Superintendent of city schools in 1860.

Rev. John F. Brooks, and A. W. Estabrook, Esq., were also early teachers, and for years were teaching at the Springfield Academy. Mr. Brooks opened a select school for young ladies on "Science Hill," South Fifth street, and Mr. Estabrook assumed control of the Third Ward School.

The first school in Springfield was taught by Andrew Orr, in 1821. Erastus Wright, Esq., followed him; and he was succeeded by Hon. Thomas Moffitt. The school at that time, numbered about 50 pupils. His last term was in the old original court house. In 1828, a school house of rough logs was built near the corner of Adams and Second streets. This building also served for a church and other public purposes. Mr. John B. Watson taught here until 1834. In 1830, Hon. John Calhoun conducted a school in another part of the city. After that time several small private schools were established, by Miss Jane C. Bergen, and Miss Chapin, and until March 1st, 1839, were the only schools in the city. Beaumont Parks, Esq., taught a private school from 1840 to 1853.

During the session of 1839 a joint stock association was formed, and the act to incorporate the "Springfield Academy" passed and approved. The following gentlemen constituted the first Board of Directors: Washington Iles, F. Webster, Jr., S. T. Logan, J. F. Rague, N. H. Ridgley, Robt. Allen and Charles R. Matheny. Under their direction a fine brick building, on 5th, between Market and Monroe streets, was built and at once opened. In the fall of 1840, Rev. John F. Brooks, who was a thorough instructor, took charge of it. In 1863 the school ceased to exist.

The Southern University was removed from Hillsboro and located here in 1852, with 166 pupils. Rev. Francis Springer was elected President, and served until the fall of 1855. The University, after many trials, is again in successful operation. It is hoped this institution will be again placed on a firm and reliable footing. Mr. W. Faucher, an energetic and well qualified teacher, now has charge of it.

By an amended charter, approved March 2, 1854, the city was erected into the Springfield School District, and the city council authorized to establish and maintain free schools, for the education of all white persons between the ages of five and twenty-one. It was also empowered to appoint a board of seven school inspectors. In accordance with this charter, an ordinance carrying it into effect was passed August 21, 1854. Preparations for erecting schools were at once made, and the First and Third Ward school houses completed in the spring, and opened the 14th of April, 1856. The First Ward was under the control of Mr. Springer, the Third Ward under A. W. Esterbrook, Esq. The other ward schools were carried on in the basements of the Baptist and First Presbyterian churches.

At a meeting of the School Board, July 16, 1857, it was determined to confine instruction in the ward schools to the common English branches, and to recommend the formation of a High School.

The school buildings in the Second and Third Wards were completed and opened, the 20th of September, 1858. Twenty-two teachers were at that time employed. In November of the same year the office of City Superintendent of Schools was created, and G. M. Cutcheon appointed to that position. At a meeting of the School Board, held December 21, 1858, it was determined to establish a school for colored children. A building on North Fifth street was procured, and Mr. Thomas York took charge of the school. Its session began January 10, and embraced 13 pupils.

The School Board, in full session, on the 27th of July 1857, established the City High School. Beaumont Parks, Esq., was appointed Principal; the school was organized and held in a small building. In 1858 it was transposed to the Fourth Ward school house.

The High School Building.

The present High School building was commenced and completed in the summer of 1865, at a cost to the city of $65,000. It is certainly one of the finest and most substantial buildings of the kind in the State, and is indeed an ornament to our city.

The city now contains one magnificent High School building, four good ward school houses, and a flourishing school for colored children, which numbers about 110 pupils. The High School is one of the best institutions of learning in the State. Its course of study is thorough and complete, comprising all the higher branches taught in any public school. It is in the hands of competent instructors, and its influence is decidedly beneficial. Below will be found the names of Principals of schools and the average attendance at each :

High School.—Prof. E. P. Frost, Principal. Three assistants. Average number of pupils attending, 180.

First Ward—J. O. Sampson, Principal. Six assistants. Average number of pupils, 380.

Second Ward—A. J. Smith, Principal. Ten assistants. Average number of pupils, 602.

Third Ward—C. F. Wilcutt, Principal. Seven assistants. Average number of pupils, 480.

Fourth Ward—James A. Mitchell. Principal. Ten assistants. Average number of pupils, 620.

Colored School—Miss M. F. Jones, Principal. One assistant. Number of pupils, 110.

The School Board is as follows : Hon. A. L. Knapp, President, Dr. John L. Million, John O. Rames, Hon. Wm. E. Shutt, Charles A. Helmle, Charles Ridgley, Dr. T. W. Dresser, Rev. J. K. McLean and Dr. B. M. Griffith.

The City Superintendent is J. C. Bennett, Esq., a gentleman of rare attainments, a most successful teacher, and an energetic business man. In his hands are the interests of the city schools well placed. His administration will redound to his honor, and the profit of the cause of education in our city. The teachers of the city schools are well worthy the positions assigned them and the trust bestowed. They will compare with any teachers in any city east or west. Under these auspices who can doubt the prosperity and influence of our school system, who can question its great and valuable workings? No one can, but must reach the conclusion that our public schools are the brightest jewels in the crown of Springfield's glory.

INDEPENDENT EDUCATIONAL INSTITUTIONS.

BETTIE STUART INSTITUTE.

Numerous efforts have been made in Springfield, at various periods of its existence, to establish an institution of learning, in which the daughters of its citizens, after having availed themselves of all the advantages to be derived from the common schools, could pursue their studies in the higher branches of learning without passing away from the parental guardianship.

In the early part of 1868,Mrs. M. McKee Homes opened a private boarding and day school for young ladies and children. The building in which her school opened was not suitable for the purpose, but she organized each department in regular order at the beginning, with a corps of eight teachers, and during the first year admitted seventy-five pupils. The citizens of Springfield were not slow to perceive Mrs. Homes' ability to manage an institution for the education of their daughters, and began to feel the imperative necessity of providing suitable buildings to accommodate the school.

To accomplish this, a few of the public-spirited citizens, in the month of July, 1869, effected an organization under the general laws of the State of Illinois for the incorporation of academies. About this time it became known that the residence of C. C. Brown, Esq., could be obtained upon very advantageous terms for such a purpose. Funds were raised to the amount of $25,000, the property secured, and measures taken to erect the necessary additional buildings. The institution was named for Mrs. C. C. Brown, deceased, who was a daughter of the Hon. John T. Stuart, and in memory of her it was called the BETTIE STUART INSTITUTE.

With the addition of the new building, the entire edifice is ninety feet front, seventy-five feet deep and two and a half stories high, making as symmetrical a home for a young ladies' collegiate institute as though it had originally been designed for the purpose. It has capacito to accommodate about two hundred pupils.

The second year, the average attendance was nearly doubled and the number of instructors increased to eleven. The institntion is now in the last half of the third year, and is increasing in usefulness and efficiency. All the teachers and a limited number of the pupils board in the institution, where they are under the influences of a Christian Home.

The ability of the instructors, the methods of teaching and the high standard of scholarship, place the Bettie Stuart Institute on an equality with the best schools for young ladies in the west. The first term of each year commences on the first Wednesday in September, which for the current year is the sixth day of the month. Persons wishing to know more of the school, can do so by addressing either of the following board of trustees. Hon. John T. Stuart, John Williams, Esq., Jacob Bunn, Esq., Hon. J. C. Conkling, John A. Chesnut, Esq., G. W. Chatterton, Esq., Dr. A. W. French, Gov. John M. Palmer, or Mrs. M. McKee Homes, Principal, Springfield, Ill.

SPRINGFIELD BUSINESS COLLEGE.

This institution has been in operation about eight years. During that time hundreds of young men have pursued the necessary studies within its walls to enable them to pass immediately from the College into the arena of business and keep accurate records. An extended scholarship in this College is good in any school of the great "International Business College Association."

The present proprietor, Mr. S. Bogardus, is a graduate of the Illinois State Normal University, at Bloomington, which is the best guaranty that he is well qualified for the discharge of the duties he has assumed.

All the common English branches are taught in this College, but when the preparatory studies have been successfully pursued. Special attention is given to the full Commercial Course, in which the following branches are represented, viz: Stock and Partners, Jobbing and Importing, Farming, Administrator's Business, Commission, Forwarding and Receiving, Steamboating, Railroading and Banking. We find the College has offices fitted up for the transaction of various branches of business, and after the student has mastered the theoretical work, he or she opens and transacts a month's business and closes one set of books in retail transactions, one in jobbing and importing, and one in commission and forwarding, with real merchandize, as it is done in *practical business.*

Besides the above, there is a partial course to accommodate those whose circumstances do not admit of their taking a full course.

Telegraphy is taught, not in theory only, but practically, with the best of instuments. The learner is taught to send and receive communication, take down, clean and set up a battery, and all other information necessary to qualify him for managing an office.

In short, a young man with the necessary preparatory studies and of ordinary labilities, after taking a full course in this institution, has a capital that wili enable him to enter successfully upon almost any branch of business.

The utility of a good, thorough school of this kind is acknowledged by all reliable business men, and the citizens of Springfield may well be proud of their own Business College.

SAINT JOSEPH'S URSULINE CONVENT

Was established in the year 1855, at the corner of Mason and Fifth streets. The buildings were burned in the winter of 1868. A new location was secured, outside the city limits, on the line of North Fifth street, and in 1866 a fine large edifice was erected, at a cost for grounds and buildings of about $75,000.

It has in regular attendance from fifty to seventy-five scholars, and from ten to twelve teachers.

Rev. Mother Mary Joseph, Lady Superior.

LUTHERAN UNIVERSITY.

This institution was organized in 1847 at Hillsboro, Montgomery county, and chartered by the General Assemby that winter. It was denominated the Hillsboro Collegiate and Theological Institute. Rev. Francis Springer, of this city, was elected President, and served until 1855. In 1852 the college was removed to Springfield, and the present college building erected at a cost of $30,000. Upon the resignation of Mr. Springer, Rev. Mr. Harkey succeeded, and acted as President until he was succeeded by Rev. W. M. Reynolds, D. D., who terminated his connection with the institution in 1855. Owing to the division in the Lutheran church, this college has been seriously embarrassed and its workings materially impeded. It is hoped, however, that these troubles will soon terminate, and that the University will be again placed on a firm basis. Mr. W. Fychon, a teacher of much merit and experience, now has charge of the educational department, and is well qualified to discharge the duties of the position.

BENEVOLENT INSTITUTIONS OF SPRINGFIELD.

THE SPRINGFIELD HOME FOR THE FRIENDLESS.

By Mr. J. A. Chesnut.

The origin of this institution may be traced to a conversation in the year 1862, between two citizens of Springfield, both now deceased. In that conversation Dr. Lathrop said to Hon. Antrim Campbell that he knew of fifty children in one neighborhood, within the city, needing charitable aid. This information moved the ever charitable mind of Mr. Campbell to seek and put in operation some plan of relief for these and other children of the city in like condition.

Mr. Campbell, to carry out the plan of relief he had matured, applied to the Legislature for an act to incorporate a board of lady managers of an institution with the above title. The act was duly passed, and approved on the 12th of Feb'y, 1863.

The ladies named in the act who were to serve as managers until the first Monday in January, 1864, were: Mrs. Eliza Pope, Mrs. Mercy Conkling, Mrs. Louisa Draper, Mrs. Susan Cook, Mrs. Lydia Williams, Mrs. Elizabeth Bunn, Mrs. Harriet Campbell, Miss Ann Eastman, Mrs. Maria Lathrop, Mrs. Mary Hay, Mrs. Catharine Hickox, Mrs. Mary Ann Dennis and Mrs. Elizabeth Matheny.

The act of incorporation made Hon. S. H. Treat, first President; Geo. Passfield, sr., first Vice-President; Geo. P. Bowen, first Secretary; and Jacob Bunn, first Treasurer.

The second section of the charter declares the object of the incorporation to be "the relieving, aiding and providing homes for friendless and indigent women and children."

Any person may become an annual member by payment of one dollar; and may become a life member by payment of ten dollars at one time.

The corporation is authorized to receive and hold, either by gift, purchase, devise, bequest or otherwise, any real or personal estate in aid of its objects.

The board of managers is the legal guardian of all children placed in its charge, according to the charter, and may bind them out to any honorable trade or employment.

The father, if living and crippled, may surrender his child to the Home. If he has absconded, or is otherwise incapable, the mother can make the surrender.

In certain cases, the Judge of a Court of Record, the Mayor of the city of Springfield, or any justice of the peace within the city, may make such surrender.

This is not a Home exclusively for *orphan children*, but for *friendless and indigent* children. It is not intended to be a permanent Home, but a place of temporary refuge and provision, and until other good homes can be procured for them.

The first meeting under the act of incorporation was held at the residence of Hon. J. C. Conkling, on the 9th March, 1863. At this meeting both Judge Treat and Mr. Passfield declined the offices for which they had been named in the charter; thereupon S. H. Melvin was elected President, and James Campbell Vice-President.

The board being now organized, began arrangements for procuring ground and building. Major E. Iles donated an entire square on South Grand Avenue, between 7th and 8th streets. A subscription was started among the citizens, and the sum of $5,620 was obtained. This was supplemented by a contribution from the city of $2,000, and by the county of Sangamon $5,000.

In the spring of 1864, a building committee was appointed, consisting of Antrim Campbell, Col. John Williams, John S. Bradford, J. S. Vredenburg, John Armstrong and John A. Chesnut. At the request of this committee, Mr. E. E. Myers, architect of this city, prepared a design and drawings for a building, which was approved by the committee.

The building is three stories, with Mansard roof—is of brick, tasty proportions, and well built. It affords accommodations for about 200 children.

The house was finished and occupied early in the year 1865. The value of the ground was estimated at $8,000, and the entire cost of the building was about $20,000. The house was erected under the superintendence of Messrs. Sutton and Runyon.

In the year 1868 Mrs. R. E. Goodell asked and obtained leave to lay out the grounds into walks, and to ornament them with shrubbery—all of which was handsomely done. While she took the leading part in this improvement, she received assistance from other citizens. The grounds are now beautifully ornamented, and the streets, on every side, set with elm shade trees. The house is supplied with water from the city water works.

On the first of May, 1864, the managers opened "The Home" in a rented house, on North Fifth street. Mrs. Nancy M. Britton was the first matron. About 60 children were received, and most of them placed in homes during the first year.

The Home has now been open for just seven years, and there have been between 900 and 1000 children received into it. There are, at this date, 31 children. Besides these, the greater number of those received have been placed in homes of comfort and positions of thrift and usefulness. Some have died, some have been taken away by their families, and a few have preferred the freedom of out door life, and have departed without leave.

There are, at present, in the Home, eight aged and otherwise indigent women, some of whom have been its inmates for years.

The benefits of this institution have been quite beyond measurement by the dollars and cents employed in its erection and the support of its helpless inmates. It requires an average of $4,000, per annum, to meet its current expenses. This involves a heavy responsibility upon the officers and managers. It requires work; but that has been cheerfully given. The Board of Supervisors of the county has treated the Institution with generosity. Every year they have voted considerable sums in aid of it. Indeed, it is doubtful whether it could have been sustained through these years without their friendly aid. The ladies deserve great credit for their enterprise in getting up fairs and in procuring private subscriptions, etc. Much has been contributed to its treasury by musical concerts, lectures, etc., etc. The public, pretty generally, have acted towards it as if the little ones in the Home were their respective wards. Some mechanics have made liberal donations on their bills, for work done—especially is this true of Mr. R. B. Zimmerman. Dr. Townsend, Dr. Barrell and Dr. Roman have bestowed faithful professional services, without a dollar of compensation. A benevolent lady of this city is putting up window blinds at this time, which will cost several hundred dollars. Mr. Thomas Strawbridge, Mr. George Judd and Mrs. Mary Lyons have been very liberal in their contributions. And these are only a few of those who have distinguished themselves in the same way.

Mrs. James C. Conkling has been one of the managers, from the first to this present day, and has ever borne a most responsible and pains-taking part. The present Board of Managers consists of the following ladies: Mrs. J. C. Conkling, Mrs. J. A. Chesnut, Mrs. Louisa Dresser, Mrs. R. B. Zimmerman, Mrs. J. Stonebarger, Mrs. N. V. Hunt, Mrs. J. Bunn, Mrs. Wm. Jayne, Mrs. Isaac Keys, Mrs. Jacob Foster, Mrs. J. D. Wickersham, Mrs. Joseph Wallace, Mrs. John Prather, Mrs. Harvey Edwards, Miss A. Clinton, Mrs. Mary Lyons, Mrs. J. D. Roper, Miss Sue Bradford, Mrs. B. H. Ferguson, Mrs. Dr. Townsend, Mrs. C. W. Matheny, Mrs. R. P. Abell, Mrs. R. D. Lawrence and Mrs. L. H. Coleman.

The officers are: S. H. Melvin, President; J. A. Chesnut, Vice-President; J. S. Bradford, Treasurer; J. W. Lane, Secretary.

There is, at present, a vacancy in the office of matron. Miss S. M. Doane is the teacher, and has present charge of the Institution.

HOME FOR FALLEN WOMEN.

Nearly every reader of these pages has heard of George Muller, and how he has sustained his Orphans' Home in England, for so many years, without asking aid from any human being. It inspires us with more exalted ideas of the ever-merciful Father, to contemplate the life of faith and prayer that is brought into exercise while thus engaged. Few, comparatively, of the citizens of Springfield are aware that a similar work has been progressing in their midst for more than three years. It is for their information that I write this article.

Having learned that there was an institution in the city for the purposes indicated by the heading of this article, I sought out the Christian gentlemen who, I was told, could give me all the information on the subject. He said he wished to have a little time to think. It was then mutually agreed that he should prepare a written statement and drop it in the post office, to my address. He did that which was more gratifying to my feelings by delivering it in person.

I ran my eye over the paper and then asked, "Who are these six friends of fallen humanity that inaugurated this work?" He replied substantially and somewhat diffidently, "that it would probably be more agreeable to their feelings not to be named, and, consulting his own feelings, it would be decidedly preferable to leave all nameless; that whatever good had been done, the honor belonged not to men but to God."

On being assured that my only aim was to mention the work in such a way as to enlist others who had not given any aid, and that I wished to say just what would be agreeable to the founders of the Institution, it was definitely settled that no names were to be mentioned.

As he was about leaving the room, I suppose he thought of the noble Christian woman who is laboring with such unselfish devotion to elevate her fallen sisters, and turning half round, said: "There is the matron ———." Then, as if the thought of mentioning no names returned, he passed out.

They ask none but God for help; it may be that He expects *you* to respond for Him. That is for *you* to decide, after reading the statement below. Although no names are given, if you desire to assist you can easily find the location of the

HOME AND HOSPITAL FOR FALLEN WOMEN,

"Situated at the south-east corner of Twelfth and Cass streets. This place of refuge was found to be a necessity, by a few persons who had been led to visit the houses of sin in our city, to tell the glad tidings of salvation to those who had fallen, by their own and others' sins, into this fearful and abandoned position.

These girls, most of them young, were without any settled place of abode, having forfeited their homes by their own acts; they now looked forward only to a life of increasing wickedness, dissipation, degradation, and a hopeless eternity.

Some were found who longed to get back into a better life. In order to do this they must have a home to start from—a home that would be to them all that their their own should have been—a good mother to care for, instruct, nurse, and again bring them back to a love of virtue and to God, and above all lead them to Jesus, who is able to save to the uttermost all who come to God by him. In this way, only, could they be fitted to return to their homes, or make an honorable living elsewhere, become useful in life and happy forever, instead of being a curse to themselves and the world.

With the view of providing this indispensable aid to these vicious and neglected girls, whom the Saviour loves, six of His and their friends, without society or organization, bought this pleasant home and ample grounds, and on the 4th of May, 1868, had it comfortably furnished and opened, to receive all of this class who would come with proper motives.

This Home has also been a lying-in hospital for children born out of wedlock, and by this means has almost invariably saved those young, often cruelly deceived mothers, from a life of open shame.

Since opening, our Home has been twice enlarged and another building rented, and at times all have been full. Since the purchase of the building no one but God has been asked for a dollar, and yet we have lacked nothing. Every want has been supplied and every anxiety removed—all has been voluntarily given. God has, through this humble Home, brought many weary souls from a life of shame into his own rest, and has said to many here, "Go, and sin no more."

The total number received during our three years existence has been two hundred and thirty-five. Of these one hundred and eighty were women, the principal part of whom were under twenty years of age. Fifty-five children have been inmates of the Home, twenty-five of whom were born there, and all except two illegitimate.

The family has averaged thirty persons from the beginning. A majority of those who have been members of our family are doing well, many of whom have been returned to their friends. Several have married, and others are making good livings, in different occupations, by their own efforts.

Our hospital department has been gratuitously attended by two of our city physicians, and medicines have been gratuitously furnished by one of our city druggists."

PUBLIC LIBRARIES.

SPRINGFIELD LIBRARY ASSOCIATION

Was incorporated under the general laws of the State, March 15, 1866. The library was opened to subscribers Feb. 23, 1869, with a catalogue of 1,300 volumes. The number of books now in the library is about 3,500. The amount of money expended in the purchase of books and fitting up the library is something over $5,000. Dr. Samuel Willard was librarian from the time it was opened until Sept. 1, 1870, when he resigned, and Miss. E. Gertrude Seaman was chosen to occupy that position.

The capital stock authorized by the articles of association is $20,000. Fifty dollars paid at one time constitutes the person paying the same a life member, and secures the use of the Library, and one vote during life. Shares of stock are ten dollars. A stock holder can have the use of the Library and one vote, by paying three dollars annually. Persons who are neither stock holders or life members can have the use of it by paying five dollars annually. The selection of books includes the very choicest works of reference, history, geography and travels, biography, theology, ethics, ecclesiastical history, philosophy, political science and education, science and art, poetry and drama, novels, juvenile works and general literature.

The directors are Charles Ridgely, E. F. Leonard, George N. Black, F. H. Wines, B. M. Griffith and C. L. Conkling.

The officers are Geo. P. Bowen, Pres't; George H. Harlow, Vice Pres't.; Tingley S. Wood, Treasurer; Samuel T. Dresser, Recording Secretary; Calvin H. Flower, Corresponding Secretary; Miss E. Gertrude Seaman, Librarian.

GERMAN READING ASSOCIATION

Was founded in 1866, and has four thousand volumes in the library, principally in the German language. H. Weisel is the Librarian.

CATHOLIC INSTITUTE ASSOCIATION.

The Catholic Institute Association and Debating Society, was organized in 1868. The library contains over one thousand standard works, comprising many rare and valuable publications, and constant additions are being made thereto.

The Library Club numbers fifty members, and holds its sessions weekly. The Association, also, has fifty members.

The following are the officers of the Association: William White, President; J. A. Kennedy and Ed. Ryan, Vice Presidents; Richard Barry, Recording Secretary; Charles Crowley, Corresponding Secretary; P. O'Connor, Treasurer; Thomas ullen, Librarian; P. J. Rourke, Agent.

ILLINOIS STATE LIBRARY.

This Library is designed for the use of the officers of State, members of the Legislature, etc., they being the only parties allowed to take books away from the Library. Any citizen, however, can visit the Library and consult any work there.

It contains 2,536 volumes of miscellaneous works, and about 7,000 volumes of the publications of the United States and of the several States, including copies of all the publications of Illinois. This makes the library proper about 10,000 volumes. These, with surplus copies of Illinois publications and incomplete sets of duplicate miscellaneous works, swell the number to 38,142 volumes, in the care of the Librarian.

The catalogue of miscellaneous books comprise some choice selections of works of reference, history, biography, philosophy, science and art, and a small number of volumes in the German language.

The State department contains the colonial laws of many of the old thirteen States; laws of the Territory and State of Illinois; laws of the Congress of the United States, with Senate and House reports; reports of the United States census; Congressional Globe, etc., etc. This library is at present in a room on the first floor of the old State House, at the west side, and is in the custody of the Hon. Edward Rummel, Secretary of State, who is *ex officio* State Librarian.

THE LAW LIBRARY

Is the property of the State also. It is in the old State House, on the first floor and the north-east corner room. It contains about 5,000 volumes, composed of the reports of the United States Courts, and of the Supreme Courts of the several States; text books, digests and statutes, and English, Irish and Scotch reports.

There is also a great number of Congressional Documents, American Archives, Secret Journals of Congress, and a small number of miscellaneous books, among which are Appleton's Cyclopedia and the Encyclopedia Brittanica. This Library is also in the care of the Secretary of State.

BENEVOLENT ORGANIZATIONS AND THEIR OFFICERS.

MASONIC BODIES.

Springfield No. 4.—R. J. Coats, W. M.; Henson Robinson, S. W.; Geo. Edwards, J. W.; Wm. Lavely, T.; J. B. Hammond, Secy.; L. F. Dyson, S. D.; Jno. Smith, J. D.; Jas. Watson, Tyler.

Central No. 71.—Chas. Fisher, W. M.; C. C. Cromwell, S. W.; Richard Young, J. W.; N. Bateman, T.; Harry C. Watson, Secy.; Z. A. Enos, S. D.; J. H. Fancher, J. D.; J. Watson, Tyler.

Tyrian No. 333.—J. C. Reynolds, W. M.; S. H. Claspill, S. W.; B. W. Ayers, J. W.; O. H. Miner, T.; John B. Saye, Sec.; John F. Burrill, S. D.; J. D. Myers, J. D.; J. Watson, Tyler.

St. Paul's No. 500.—L. H. Bradley, W. M.; A. L. Knapp, S. W.; B. S. Edwards, J. W.; John Peters, T.; E. R. Roberts, Secy.; J. F. McNeil, S. D.; J. Bradley, J. D.; J. Watson, Tyler.

Springfield Royal Arch Chapter No. 1.—John F. Burrill, H. P.; Richard Young, K.; J. McBurnett, S.; S. H. Claspill, C. of H.; Z. A. Enos, P. S.; R. S. McGuire, S.; Wm. Lavely, T.

Springfield Council No. 2.—J. C. Reynolds, T. I. G. M.; R. J. Coats, Dept. T. I. G. M.; J. F. Burrill, P. C. W.; O. H. Miner, T.; John B. Saye, Secy.; B. F. Caldwell, Capt. of Guard; S. H. Claspill, Cond'r; A. R. Robinson, Sentinel.

Elwood Commandary No. 6, *K. T.*—R. L. McGuire, E. C.; J. B. Hammond, Gens.; W. A. Turney, C. G.; L. B. Smith, Recorder; J. S. Fisher, T.; Richard Young, S. W.; T. G. Gorman, S. W.; J. L. Crane, Prelate; L. Rosette, Warden; Dwight Brown, S. B.; John P. Baker, Sword Bearer; G. Burkhardt, Sentinel.

ODD FELLOWS ORGANIZATIONS.

Sangamon Lodge No. 6.—Wm. Stadden, N. G.; W. A. Duggins, V. G.; H. O. Bolles, R. S.; J. D. Roper, P. S.; John A. Hughes, T.; Ed. Henderson, W.; Chas. Freitag, I. G.; John Wolfe, O. G.; Wm. Kirby, Conductor.

I. O. O. F.—Teutonia Lodge.—Joseph Saul, N. G.; Jacob Eberlin, V. G.; Fred. Weiss, R. Secy.; S. Hecht, P. Secy.; G. Burkhardt, Treas.

Prairie State Encampment No. 16.—J. D. Roper, C. P.; S. J. Willett, H. P.; John Wolfe, S. W.; John A. Hughes, J. W.; L. F. Dyson, Scribe; J. C. Beam, T.

Knights of Pythias—Capitol Lodge No. 14.—J. D. Roper, W. C.; S. J. Willett, V. C.; E. N. Dangerfield, V. P.; J. H. Hull, R. S.; A. T. Smith, F. S.; John A. Hughes, B.; A. E. Rae, I. S.: C. DeCamp, O. S.; A. E. Henkle, G.; S. J. Willett, J. B. Hammond and J. L. Hudson, Trustees.

Brotherhood of Locomotive Engineers—Division No. 23.—George R. Hough, C.; H. Button, F. E.; E. T. Harris, S. E.; P. Teal, F. A. E.; A. Marney, S. A. E.; H. Hamilton, T. A. E.; J. M. Smith, Guide; B. Mallard, Chaplin.

Emmis Lodge No. 67, *Independent Order Beni Berith.*—L. Benjamin, Pres't; R. Springer, V. P.; S. Rosenwald, M.; S. Redlich, A. M.; M. Myers, W.; M. A. Long, Secy; G. Frisch, T.; M. Myers, S. Rosenwald and M. A. Long, Trustees.

SOME OF THE PUBLIC AND PRIVATE BUILDINGS, WITH THE COST OF CONSTRUCTION.

UNITED STATES BUILDINGS.

Court House and Post Office ...$320,000

STATE INSTITUTIONS.

The Governor's Mansion $100,000
State Arsenal and grounds..... 25,000

COUNTY BUILDINGS.

Court House ....$ 16,000
County Jail 7,570

CITY IMPROVEMENTS.

South Market, corner Fourth and Monroe streets..............$ 40,000
North Market, corner Fifth and Madison streets.............. 22,000
City Hall and Lot............ 7,000
First Ward Engine House 5,000
Second Ward Engine House.... 10,000
High School................. 65,000
1st, 2d, 3d and 4th Ward School Houses, $25,000 each 100,000

The following list gives the cost of the churches and independent school buildings:

CHURCHES.

First Presbyterian.......................$30,000 00
Second " 80,000 00
Third " 65,000 00
Congregational......................... 18,000 00
Episcopal.............................. 28,000 00
First Baptist.......................... 20,000 00
Second " 15,000 00
First Methodist........................ 30,000 00
Second " 7,000 00
Church of Immaculate Conception...... 30,000 00
Church of St. Paul and St. Peter 20,000 00

SCHOOLS AND COLLEGES.

St. Ursuline Convent.................. 75,000 00
Bettie Stuart Institute................. 40,000 00
St. Paul's College and grounds.......... 30,000 00

RESIDENCES.

Hon. B. S. Edwards...........$ 50,000
Ex-Gov. J. A. Matteson 150,000
Hon. J. C. Conkling 50,000
C. M. Smith 45,000
C. W. Matheny................$ 30,000
S. H. Melvin 20,000
Hon. S. T. Logan 30,000
Jesse K. Dubois 25,000
David Littler................ 30,000
Col. John Williams........... 20,000
Jacob Bunn 35,000
Thos. Ragsdale 30,000
Wesley Kimber................ 25,000
O. M. Sheldon................ 20,000
Geo. W. Chatterton........... 20,000
Isaac H. Gray................ 18,000
John H. Johnson.............. 30,000
O. M. Hatch.................. 20,000
E. S. Fowler................. 20,000
Hon. J. A. McClernand........ 20,000
G. A. Sutton................. 20,000
Hon. S. M. Cullom 20,000
Geo. M. Brinkerhoff.......... 35,000
N. H. Ridgely................ 45,000
E. L. Baker 45,000
James L. Lamb 30,000
J. A. Chesnut................ 50,000
W. A. Turney 20,000
Mrs. G. Jayne 10,000
S. H. Jones 20,000
B. Stuvè..................... 20,000
C. A. Gehrmann............... 20,000
John Cook 25,000
Jacob Foster 10,000
A. J. Babcock 8,000
Dr. John Brown............... 8,000
T. S. Little................. 15,000
W. B. Corneau................ 18,000
Geo. Woods................... 20,000
R. Rudolph 18,000
Mrs. N. Strott 15,000
C. E. Lippincott............. 12,000
L. Smith..................... 10,000
Robt. Officer 12,000
Hon. J. H. Beveridge......... 12,000

T. J. Dennis	$ 12,000
Geo. L. Huntington	15,000
J. T. Smith	20,000
Hon. N. W. Edwards	45,000
B. F. Fox	30,000
Hon. N. Bateman	10,000
H. N. Edwards	10,000
Geo. N. Black	20,000
John E. Roll	10,000
R. M. Ridgely	10,000
Mrs. E. Wright	10,000
Hon. A. Starne	15,000
E. Payne	10,000
Dr. Wm. Jayne	18,000
Hon. E. Rummel	10,000
Noah Mason	12,000
Wiley Brasfield	10,000
Hon. Wm. Butler	20,000
Speed Butler	15,000
Hon. Sharon Tyndale	15,000
R. F. Ruth	15,000
D. L. Phillips	25,000

Below will be found a few of the fine buildings recently erected in the county:

COUNTRY RESIDENCES.

Jacob Foster	$ 10,000
W. B. Huffaker	28,000
David A. Brown	15,000
Dewitt Smith	10,000
George Merriman	10,000
George Turley	10,000

HOTELS.

Leland	$350,000
St. Nicholas	100,000
Chenery	40,000
Revere	40,000
American	40,000
Western	35,000
Everett	35,000

Annexed will be found the valuation of the principal public buildings of Springfield:

BANKS.

Springfield Marine and Fire Ins.	$ 50,000
J. Bunn's Banking House	45,000
Springfield Savings Bank	25,000
Ridgely National Bank	25,000
First National Bank	20,000
State National Bank	20,000

BUSINESS BLOCKS.

Kimber & Ragsdale, Adams st.	$ 60,000
Conkling's, Monroe, bet. 4th and 5th sts	65,000
Conkling's, cor. Monroe and 5th	20,000
Cook's, 6th, between Adams and Washington	45,000
Cook's, Monroe, bet. 5th and 6th	25,000
Keuchler, Edwards & Ferguson	40,000
Carpenter's	30,000
S. T. Logan's	20,000
Harts, Bates & Kimball	30,000
Springer's	50,000
E. L. Baker's	30,000

CHARITABLE INSTITUTIONS.

Home for the Friendless, building and grounds	$ 30,000

FOUNDRIES.

Ætna, J. C. Lamb	$ 40,000
Excelsior, Berryman & Rippon.	25,000

MANUFACTORIES.

Springfield Watch Factory	$ 75,000
Springfield Woolen Factory	75,000
Springfield Planing Mill	40,000
Booth & Son, Wagon Factory	40,000
Withey & Bro., Wagon Factory	30,000

PLACES OF AMUSEMENT.

Springfield Opera House	$125,000
Springfield Skating Rink	16,000

OFFICERS OF THE UNITED STATES, STATE, COUNTY AND CITY, TRANSACTING BUSINESS IN SPRINGFIELD.

UNITED STATES OFFICERS.

Judge U. S. Supreme Court, assigned to 7th Circuit.—Hon. David Davis, Bloomington.

Judge U. S. Circuit Court. — Hon Thomas Drummond, Chicago.

Judge of United States Court.—Hon. Samuel H. Treat, Springfield.

Marshal.—John L. Routt.

Assistant.—J. E. Hill.

Clerk District Court.—Geo. P. Bowen.

Clerk Circuit Court.—John A. Jones.

Attorney.—Bluford Wilson.

Register in Bankruptcy. — Lawrence Weldon.

United States Commissioners.— L. B. Adams, Geo. P. Bowen, F. W. Cole, A. W. Wood, M. B. Converse.

Assessor.—Edward L. Baker.

Assistants.—John P. Baker and Jesse W. Bice.

Chief Clerk.—B. W. Briggs.

Collector.—John T. Harper.

Deputy Collector.—H. C. Latham.

Chief Clerk.—A. L. Smith.

Pension Agent.—W. Jayne.

Chief Clerk.—T. W. Chenery.

Register of the Land Office.—W. F. Elkin.

Receiver of the Land Office.—George N. Black.

Post Master.—J. L. Crane.

Chief Clerk.—S. B. Moody.

Custodian U. S. Court House.—E. L. Baker.

Janitor.—A. R. Robinson.

UNITED STATES COURTS.

Circuit Court.—Regular Terms : First Monday of January and first Monday of June.

District Court.—Regular Terms : First Monday of January and first Monday of June.

Special Admiralty Terms.—First Monday of every month.

SUPREME COURT JUDGES.

Chief Justice.—Charles R. Lawrence.

Judges.—Hon. Sidney Breese, Carlyle; Hon. Pinkney Walker, Rushville; Hon. John M. Scott, Bloomington ; Hon. J. K. McAllister, Chicago; Hon. Benjamin R. Sheldon, Galena; Hon. Anthony Thornton, Shelbyville.

Clerk.—Wm. A. Turney, Springfield.

STATE OFFICERS.

Governor.—John M. Palmer.

Lieut.-Governor.—John Dougherty.

Secretary of State.—E. Rummel.

Auditor.—Chas. E. Lippincott.

Treasurer.—E. N. Bates.

Superintendent of Public Instruction.—Newton Bateman.

Adjutant-General.—H. Dilger.

Assistant Secretary of State.—Geo. H. Harlow.

Private Secretary to the Governor.—E. B. Harlan.

COUNTY OFFICERS.

Judge.—Hon. John A. McClernand.

Clerk of Circuit Court.—Chas. H. Lanphier.

Clerk of the County Court.—N. W. Matheny.

Probate Judge.—A. N. J. Crook.

Sheriff.—A. B. McConnell.

Coroner.—Ed. Bierce.

Jailor.—Martin Tincher.

Superintendent of Public Schools.—Warren A. Burgett.

CITY OFFICERS.

Mayor.—John W. Smith.

Clerk.—Frank Fleury.

Treasurer.—George W. Krodell.

Assessor and Collector.—Jas. Taylor.

Marshal.—Thomas White.

Street Supervisor.—John Nelch.

Attorney.—Thomas G. Prickett.

Comptroller.—E. R. Roberts.

Market Masters.—Wm. Alexander and Charles Lorsch.

Fire Warden.—Wm. Sands.

City Engineer.—James M. Bourne.

Aldermen.—First Ward: Frank Hudson, Frank W. Tracy, Ralph J. Coates. Second Ward: Hobert T. Ives, Maurice Fitzgerald, C. A. Helmle. Third Ward: John S. Bradford, Henry N. Alden, H. S. Dickerman. Fourth Ward: R. M. Ridgely, Obed Lewis, Lyman Sherwood.

BOARD OF TRADE.

President.—S. H. Melvin.

1st Vice-President.—J. S. Vredenburg.

2d Vice-President.—A. Nolte.

Secretary.—W. B. Cowgill.

Treasurer.—F. W. Tracy.

YOUNG MEN'S CHRISTIAN ASSOCIATION.

President.—John T. Stuart, Jr.

Recording Secretary.—Jas. Fairchild.

Treasurer.—C. J. Salter.

Vice-Presidents.—Geo. W. Ingalls and H. N. Keener, M. D.

Executive Committee.—Jno. T. Stuart, Jas. Fairchild, C. J. Salter, J. W. Ingalls, H. N. Keener, E. A. Wilson.

GRAND ARMY OF REPUBLIC.

Springfield Post.—E. B. Harlan, Post Commander; L. C. Reiner, Sr. Vice Post Com; W. P. Emery, Jr. Vice-Post Com.; G. S. Dana, Post Adjutant; D. C. Brinkerhoff, Post Quartermaster; Rev. D. F. Carnahan, Post Chaplain; N. B. Wiggins, Officer of the Day; Chas. Layton, Officer of the Guard.

BUSINESS HOUSES AND FIRMS IN SPRINGFIELD.

There is no pretensions made towards giving all the mercantile business of the city, but the following notices comprise some of the principal houses and firms:

AGRICULTURAL IMPLEMENTS.

C. R. Post sells about $65,000 worth of agricultural implements, annually. His supplies come from manufactories in New York, Michigan, Wisconsin, Indiana and Illinois. Mr. Post also buys and ships, each year, about $50,000 worth of grain. His place of business is near the depot of the T. W. & W. railway.

Frank R. McConnell deals in agricultural implements and farm machinery. His supplies are brought from Michigan, Ohio, Indiana and Illinois. His sales amount to from $40,000 to $50,000 annually. Corner Monroe and Eighth streets.

Staley & Troxell deal largely in all kinds of agricultural implements, farm machinery, and field and garden seeds. Annual sales from $25,000 to $30,000. Washington street, between Fourth and Fifth.

Besides those above named there are several other firms whose main business is dealing in agricultural implements, and still others who have them in connection with hardware stores, stove and tin ware stores, feed stores, etc., etc.

In another part of these pages will be found a statement of the aggregate amount of sales of all kinds of agricultural implements, for one year, in Springfield.

AGENTS OF ALL KINDS.

INSURANCE.

HILL & FLOWER.—Among the institutions of the city may be classed the insurance agency of Messrs. Hill & Flower, who have fine and commodious rooms just opposite the Post Office. Mr. J. S. Hill, the senior partner, is, with one exception, the oldest insurance agent in the State, having entered the business in 1836. Since 1845 Mr. Hill has been engaged in insuring in this city. His first company, which he still retains (the oldest in the State and among the best), was the Illinois Mutual. Mr. Hill is well and favorably known by all our citizens. Mr. Flower has been engaged in the insurance business since 1864. Prior to that time he was engaged in teaching school, but was compelled to abandon that occupation on account of poor health. He is a tip top business man, and deservedly popular. This firm represent the New York Mutual Life, the largest and best company in the world, also the oldest in America. Messrs. Hill & Flower also represent the following fourteen fire insurance companies, which they challenge the world to produce their equal for reliability, safety and promptness. Below will be found the list.

Ætna, Hartford, $5,738,635; City Fire, Hartford, $548,287; Hartford, Hartford, $2,737,519; Home, New York, $4,578,008; Manhattan, N. Y., $1,407,788; Market, N. Y., $704,684; Merchants, Hartford, $540,000; Merchants, Chicago, $878,252; North American, Hartford, $546,563; New York Mutual Life, gross assets nearly $45,000,000; Phœnix, Hartford, $1,738,921; Security, N. Y., $1,880,333; Springfield F. & M., Mass., $936,400.

A. W. COLEMAN is the General Agent of the Globe Mutual Life Insurance Company of New York. This company issues registered policies, which secures a guarantee from the State of New York for re-insurance in the event of a failure of the company. The Globe Mutual offers all the advantages of any other first class life insurance company, and Mr. Coleman is one of the most reliable insurance men in this part of the country. His office is on Monroe street, opposite the Post Office.

GRANT & BURRILL, in the old Post Office building, are also extensively engaged in the insurance business. Both are well known and popular agents. Their business is quite large, and they aim to give satisfaction to each and every customer. They represent nine companies—eight fire and one life. Among their fire companies is the Sangamo, a home institution of Springfield.

HUGHES & SMITH are also largely engaged in the business of insurance. They represent some of the best companies in the United States, and always adjust the losses of the companies they represent.

E. B. HAWLEY is agent for the Ætna Life Insurance Company of Hartford, one of the old established companies. It gives all the advantages any other first class company does.

THOMAS LEWIS is Manager of the Illinois State Department of the Atlas Mutual Life Insurance Company of St. Louis, Mo. This company has abolished all restrictions on travel, in any part of the world.

EXPRESS COMPANIES.

E. D. JUDD is agent for the American Merchants Union. Office on Washington street, between Fifth and Sixth.

J. W. CARTER is agent for the United States Express Company.

REAL ESTATE AGENTS AND ABSTRACT WRITERS.

EDWARD A. WILSON is the well known agent of the Charter Oak Life Insurance Company, of Hartford, Conn. For the last five years he has held that position, and in his hands the interests of the company have been well guarded and advanced, as the records of his business fully demonstrate.

Mr. Wilson is also one of our heaviest Real Estate Agents, and has now upon his books for sale over $300,000 of choice city and country property, embracing some of the most desirable property to be found in this section of the country. Parties in the East, having money to loan on first-class security, will consult their interests by transacting their business through Mr. Wilson. He can invest money in real estate worth three times the amount of loan, secured by deeds of trust, without cost to the loaner. Mr. Wilson's well-known business capacity and character afford the best guarantee that all business intrusted in his hands will meet the most careful and prompt attention.

LATHAM & ENOS.—H. C. Latham and P. P. Enos give their entire attention to buying and selling real estate, paying taxes and making abstracts of deeds. Should you desire information respecting the title of any piece of real estate in Sangamon county, they will give you every link in the chain, if it is perfect, or if there is a defect they will tell you just where it is. They are perfectly reliable. Office, Monroe street, between Fifth and Sixth.

GEN. T. S. MATHER is one of the oldest real estate and loan agents in town. He sells property, rents houses, farms, etc., pays taxes and performs all other business pertaining to the land and real estate agency. Gen. Mather was raised in Springfield and is well known by our citizens and business men, and has been carrying on the business for about seven years.

AUCTION AND COMMISSION MERCHANT.

FRANK MYERS, successor to the late firm of H. C. Myers & Son, is one of the largest auction and commission merchants in the State, outside of Chicago. The firm of H. C. Myers & Son was established in 1861, and at once became an important and enormous business. For the last thirty-five years Mr. H. C. Myers has been engaged in selling goods in Springfield, and was universally esteemed and a great favorite. Upon his decease, in January last, Mr. Frank Myers —son and surviving partner of the deceased—took entire control of the business, and is now carrying it on in a highly successful manner. The entire establishment, from the celler to the garret, is stocked with goods; and everything usually kept in such a line of business can be found on hand. The yearly sales of this house are about $100,000 and the amount of capital invested foots up $20,000.

ATTORNEYS OF SPRINGFIELD.

STUART, EDWARDS & BROWN.—Hon. John T. Stuart, Benjamin S. Edwards and Christopher C. Brown.

CULLOM, ZANE & MARCY.—Hon. Shelby M. Cullom, Chas. S. Zane and Geo. O. Marcy.

J. C. & C. L. CONKLING.—James C. Conkling and Clinton L. Conkling.

HERNDON & ORENDORFF.—Wm. H. Herndon and Alfred Orendorff.

JOHN E. ROSETTE & BRO.—John E. Rosette and L. Rosette.

HARVEY & WOLCOTT.—Charles D. Harvey and Richard Wolcott.

E. L. & W. L. GROSS.—Eugene L. Gross and William L. Gross.

MATHENY & MCGUIRE.—James H. Matheny and Robert L. McGuire.

HAY, GREENE & LITTLER.—Milton Hay, Henry S. Greene and David P. Littler.

BROADWELL & SPRINGER.—Wm. M. Springer and Norman M. Broadwell.

ROBINSON, KNAPP & SHUTT.—James C. Robinson, Anthony L. Knapp and Wm. E. Shutt.

MORRISON & PATTON.—C. M. Morrison and James W. Patton.

PRICKETT & HAMILTON.—Thomas G. Prickett and L. F. Hamilton.

BRADLEY, OLDEN & BRADLEY.—L. H. Bradley, W. P. Olden and J. K. Bradley.

CHARLES A. KEYES.

WILLIAM E. MORRISON.

CHARLES H. RICE.
WILLIAM M. FOWLER.
WILLIAM PRESCOTT.
SAMUEL D. SCHOLES.
PARKE E. TEMPLE.
J. A. KENNEDY.
J. S. STEVENS.
BERNARD STUVE.
THOMAS C. MATHER.
WM. J. CONKLING, War Claim Agent.

The bar of Springfield is admitted to be one of the most talented in the West. We append a few running remarks, with reference to individual members, and firms:

HON. JOHN T. STUART, of the firm of Stuart, Edwards & Brown, is the oldest practicing attorney in Springfield. He was the preceptor and first law partner of Abraham Lincoln, has been three times elected to Congress, is president of nearly half a dozen organizations for advancing the interests of Springfield, and still retains his position in the front rank of his profession. He is one of the few men who know how to grow old gracefully.

HON. B. S. EDWARDS is a son of Hon. Ninian Edwards, the former territorial Governor of the State and one of the first United States Senators, after Illinois was admitted into the Union. Upon the creation of Sangamon county into a judicial circuit, Judge Edwards was the first judge, having been elected without any opposition. He is a very able lawyer.

MR. C. C. BROWN, the junior member, is a thorough, honest and conscientious attorney. As a legal adviser he has but few equals at the Springfield bar.

HON. E. B. HERNDON is one of the oldest practicing lawyers in the city. He bears a high rank, and is justly considered one of the ablest minds in the legal fraternity.

HON. SHELBY M. CULLOM, of Cullom, Zane & Marcy, was one of the most faithful and energetic representatives in Congress the Eighth District ever had. He devotes the same talents and energy to his profession. Mr. Cullom is a working man, and occupies the responsible position of President of the State National Bank.

HON. JAMES C. CONKLING, senior member of the firm of J. C. & C. L. Conkling, father and son, is one of the most energetic and public spirited citizens Springfield can boast of. All public improvements meet his hearty sanction and support, and the magnificent buildings by him erected during the last five years will stand as enduring monuments of his liberal public spirit. Mr. Conkling has filled many important public positions in the State.

The firm of HERNDON & ORENDORFF is a very able one. Mr. Herndon, now growing old, was a member of the firm of Lincoln & Herndon. After the death of Mr. Lincoln he associated with him Mr. Alfred Orendorff, a young and promising attorney, who is now the active member of the firm. Herndon & Orendorff still occupy the old office of Lincoln & Herndon.

JOHN E. ROSETTE, of Rosette & Bro., is a man of talents, and justly occupies a prominent position as a member of the Springfield Bar. He is considered the best criminal lawyer in the city.

HARVEY & WOLCOTT are rapidly working their way to the head of the profession.

E. L. & W. L. GROSS are young men, who, in addition to the regular practice of the profession, commenced, in 1867, the work of compiling the Statutes of the State of Illinois, and after years of study and arduous labor, the result was a volume containing all the laws of the State then in force. By successive revisions they have brought the work down to the present time, and "Gross' Statutes" are now the official standard in all the courts,

Meeting with success in their first publication, they have continued their labors and are now furnishing the legal profession with the following works:

Index to all the Laws of the State from its Organization down to 1860.

The Criminal Code of Illinois: a Digest of Statutes and Decisions, relating to Crime and its Punishment. The Statutes and decisions under them are placed side by side.

Illinois Legal Directory: a Record of the Courts of Illinois, with the name of every practicing lawyer in the State. It is published quarterly, with corrections to date.

Organic Laws of Illinois, containing the act and deed of cession by Virginia, Ordinance of 1787, Constitution of the United States, and the three Constitutions of Illinois.

Attorney's Business Docket. It is a day-book, journal and ledger combined, and always posted.

Labeled envelopes, for filing papers; a great convenience.
the firm of Matheny & McGuire, possesses fine legal attainments, and as an orator is

Col. J. H. Matheny senior member of excelled by none in the country. He is a Springfielder, to "the manor born," and is known to nearly every person in this portion of the state.

Milton Hay, of the firm of Hay, Greene and Littler, is one of the oldest and most reliable attorneys at the bar. He was a member of the late Constitutional Convention, and left the impress of his mind upon that valuable instrument. He is a deep, earnest thinker and his legal opinion has much weight.

Judge Broadwell, of Broadwell & Springer, has held many responsible positions in public life, and filled them most acceptably. Hon. Wm. Springer is one of the representatives from this county to the General Assembly. This firm has a high position among the profession.

Robinson, Knapp & Shutt do a large amount of business. Hon. James C. Robinson is the member of Congress from this district, and has also represented the Seventh District, and is an old and efficient lawyer. Hon. A. L. Knapp has been a member of Congress, and is a gentleman of clear legal mind and ability. Hon. Wm. E. Shutt has filled the office of Mayor of the city of Springfield, and is a promising young lawyer.

Mr. C. M. Morrison, of Morrison & Patton, is Prosecuting Attorney for this district, and is an able lawyer. Mr. Patton is young, studious, and promises to occupy a good position in the profession.

Mr. Chas. A. Keyes is Master in Chancery of Sangamon county; Hon. Wm. Prescott was formerly Probate Judge; and Chas. H. Rice is one of the representatives to the General Assembly.

Besides the above mentioned names, Springfield has a number of young and promising attorneys, who are zealously working their way to the front rank in the profession. Among them are many who are truly worthy to follow in the footsteps of the illustrious lawyers who have heretofore and are now shedding such glory upon the bar of Springfield.

BANKS.

N. H. Ridgely, of this city, is probably the oldest banker in the State of Illinois, having commenced the business of banking in the year 1829, as an officer of the St. Louis branch of the United States Bank, of which Nicholas Biddle was President. He came to Springfield in 1845 to accept the office of cashier of the State Bank of Illinois. At the time of its failure he was appointed one of the trustees to wind up its affairs, which position he held until the final settlement. In 1852, he organized the Clarke Exchange Bank in this city, which was wound up in 1854, when he began private banking on his own account.

In 1858, his son Charles, and afterwards his son William, became associated with him, and the business was carried on under the firm name of N. H. Ridgely & Co. In 1866 the Ridgely National Bank was organized, with a paid up capital of $100,000, with authority to increase it to $500,000. A surplus has since been accumulated which makes the real working capital of the bank $250,000. By its last report its loans and discounts were about $500,000, and its deposits about $400,000.

In connection with this bank there is a savings department, in which deposits to any amount are received on the terms usual with savings banks, and interest allowed at the rate of six per cent. per annum. The bank also deals in foreign exchange, and latterly has been paying special attention to the purchase and sale of county, city and township bonds, and negotiation of loans on real estate.

The officers of the Ridgely National Bank are N. H. Ridgely, President; Charles Ridgely, Vice President; Wm. Ridgely, Cashier.

J. Bunn's Banking House.—Mr. Bunn is one of the oldest bankers in this section of the State, and is one of the best known business men in the city. Mr. Bunn began banking on the 1st of January, 1851, at the corner just east of his present banking house, in the building occupied by J. & J. W. Bunn, grocers. In 1858 he erected the elegant bank building which he now occupies, on the southwest corner of the square, at a cost of $25,000. The business transacted by Mr. Bunn is very large and extensive in its various ramifications.

First National Bank was organized December 12th, 1863, and commenced operations May 1st, 1864, with a capital of 125,000. The capital was increased July 1st, of the same year, to $150,000, and the following January to $200,000. On January 1st, 1871, it was increased to $400,000. It had on hand on the first day of May, 1871, a surplus fund of $65,000.

The business of this bank for the year 1870, shows an average deposit account of from $600,000 to $700,000. Amount of money loaned during the year, about $2,500,000; number of persons to whom loaned, about 800; average amount loaned to each person, $3,000, and average time, sixty days. The First National Bank pays interest on long time deposits but has no savings department. Its officers are among the best known, and most popular in the banking department. They are as follows: John Williams, President; Elijah Iles, Vice President; Frank W. Tracy, Cashier; John Williams, Elijah Iles, George N. Black, A. P. Williams, C. W. Matheny, N. W. Matheny and J. C. Henkle, Directors.

Springfield Marine and Fire Insurance Company was chartered with a clause permitting it to transact a banking business. It has never availed itself of any other provision in its charter than banking. Capital, $100,000, with a contingent fund of $90,000.

The Springfield Savings Bank was incorporated by the General Assembly of Illinois, with special rights and privileges, Feb. 28, 1867. Its capital stock was fixed by that act at $100,000.

From time immemorial, institutions for the accumulation and custody of money have been regarded as something in which the rich only were or could be interested. A century ago the thought that a man who did not count his wealth by thousands, could have been interested in a bank would have seemed preposterous. The idea originated from pure benevolence, and in all their essential features they are eleemosynary institutions. In the year 1798, some wealthy, benevolent gentleman in one of the manufacturing districts of England, voluntarily offered to receive from working people, in their neighborhood, such sums of money as could be spared from their earnings, and return the same at Christmas, with the addition of one-third of the amount. This addition was not intended as interest, for it is not likely those gentlemen made any use of it, but it was merely a bounty for economy.

The circumstance, however, suggested the thought of combining business with benevolence, and since that time Savings Banks have been established in all civilized countries. Men who have made the subject of finance a study, form corporations by subscribing sufficient stock to afford security, and then receive, from day to day and from week to week, a portion, be it small or great, of the wages of the day laborer, or any other person of limited means, giving a promise to return it at a fixed time with an additional amount as interest.

By these institutions the weak and timid are assisted to provide against future want, while the strong man, whose appetites may lead him astray, can remove the cause of temptation, and at the same time provide for future emergencies. The Springfield Savings Bank has been unusually successful from the beginning, having now more than four thousand depositors, with an aggregate balance of nearly half a million dollars, and is paying its depositors over $1000 interest every month. In addition to its Savings department it does a general banking business.

Its officers are, S. H. Melvin, President; C. A. Helmle, Vice-President; J. A. Chesnut, Cashier; T. S. Wood, As't Cashier.

STATE NATIONAL BANK.

The State National Bank was organized under the United States banking law, November 11th, 1870, and began operations January 1st, 1871.

The officers are, Hon. S. M. Cullom, President; A. M. Sims, Vice-President; S. H. Jones, Cashier; and Joseph W. Lane, Teller.

The amount of capital stock is one hundred and fifty thousand dollars, with power to increase it to one million. It is designed to increase the capital fifty thousand dollars more, on July 1st, making it then two hundred thousand dollars.

The State National, since its organization, has been steadily increasing and enlarging its business. Its workings and operations have proven most satisfactorily to its owners. The circulation of this bank is $135,000, its loans and discount $185,000, and amount of deposits for first year $100,000.

BAKERY AND CONFECTIONERY

Henry Hauck, on north Fifth street, is carrying on a first class bakery and confectionery. His business is large and growing, and he makes the best of cakes, pies, bread, etc.

Charles H. Long has a bread and cracker bakery in constant operation. He also deals in groceries, both staple and fancy, and yankee notions.

David Hickey is one of the oldest confectioners in town, and is well known to all our citizens. He has constantly on hand a choice stock of confectionaries, toys, fruits, etc., and is still in his well known bakery, South Sixth street.

Jacob Sterneman has been carrying on a bread bakery in Springfield for a number of years. He is now having a steam engine and other appropriate machinery made preparatory to putting in operation a steam cracker bakery, on an extensive scale.

BOOK STORES AND NEWS DEPOTS,

John H. Johnson.—This well known and favorite establishment is the oldest book store in the State, it having been established in the year 1837. Since that time but two changes have been made in the firm. The old firm of Johnson & Bradford was known all over Illinois, and its reputation and business standing was always A No. 1. Upon the withdrawal of Capt. Bradford, Mr. Johnson took entire control, and under his administration the house has fully sustained its high standing. He has now in store a choice and elegant stock of books and stationery, comprising everything kept in a first-class book store, and is prepared to offer special inducements to purchasers.

Capt. J. S. Bradford is one of the old landmarks in the book and stationery business in this city, having been engaged therein, in company with J. H. Johnson, since 1841, until about one year ago. The firm of Johnson & Bradford was one of the best known and popular ones in this section, and was indeed "household words." They built up an enormous trade, and were justly noted for integrity and fair business dealing. Having spent over a quarter of a century together, they concluded they were old enough to "go it alone," and they dissolved partnership over one year ago, Shortly after, Capt. Bradford opened his present elegant establishment in the old Post Office. He has now one of the best selected stocks in the city, and his large and increasing business shows the high esteem entertained for him by the people generally.

P. W. Harts commenced business in the month of October, 1865. He runs two distinct branches of mercantile business in one establishment. Having one of the finest and largest store rooms in the city, he keeps a full line of Drugs, Mèdicines and Fancy Articles on one side, and an equally fine assortment of Books and Stationery on the other. Mr. Harts is one of the most energetic and thorough-going business men in the west. His annual sales amount to about $40,-000. His store is at the south side of Capitol Square.

Mrs. Mary R. Faith keeps a book store for the sale of Catholic books, almost exclusively.

O. H. McGraw is the oldest News Dealer in the city, and from a small beginning has built up a good business. Mr. McGraw has all the late papers and publications of the day upon his counters, and is always up with the times. He also has a small and carefully selected stock of Books, and other articles in his line, and all other necessaries for a first class News Depot.

S. Brown, east side of Capitol Square, has all the late papers and periodicals. His counters are always filled with good reading matter. He has, also, a good stock of fresh Fruits and Confectionery always on hand.

BOOT AND SHOE DEALERS AND MAKERS.

Walter Ordway has been engaged for the last ten years in selling boots and shoes on the north side of the square. Mr. Ordway came from Kansas City, Mo., at the commencement of the "late unpleasantness," and opened in the small frame building now occupied by Chas. Stern, the clothier. From that beginning he has largely increased his trade, and now occupies one of the finest store rooms on the north side. His facilities for business are not surpassed. His sales amount to about $65,000 annually.

John E. Roll came to Sangamon county June 7, 1830, and settled at the town of Sangamo, where he helped Abraham Lincoln build a flat boat, which he ran out of the Sangamon river into the Illinois, and out of that into the Mississippi, and down that stream. Mr. Roll came to Springfield soon after and has been an active business man to the present time. He has done much to improve the place, having built a dozen or more of the best residences in it, besides doing a large merchantile business. He is now engaged in the boot and shoe trade with W. V. Roll & Co., north side of square

J. C. Latham, successor to Latham & Co., is very extensively engaged in the boot and shoe trade. Mr. Latham purchases his goods of the manufacturers, buys very extensively for cash, and is able to present great inducements to purchasers. His stock embraces the finest and cheapest goods, selected expressly for the trade, of this city and county. Mr. Latham has a stock of $30,000, and his yearly sales amount to about $70,000.

A. Ensel sell boots and shoes to the value of $30,000 per year. Mr. Ensel has been in the business in this city but for a short time, yet he has built up a large and growing trade.

Sims, Smith & Co. have recently engaged in selling boots and shoes, having purchased the large stock of goods recently owned by F. George & Son, north side of the square. The gentlemen composing this firm are old and prominent citizens, Capt. J. W. Smith having been sheriff of this county and mayor of the city, which position he is now holding for the third time. Sims, Smith & Co. have a large stock of goods and are constantly adding thereto, and are selling a large amount of boots and shoes.

SIDNEY LANPHEAR employs a competent corps of workmen and uses none but the best of materials. He makes every description of boots and shoes to order, and warrants satisfaction in every respect.

Mr. Lanphear holds the exclusive right to use the celebrated Plummer last. For ease, comfort and firm support to the foot, a boot or shoe made on this last is far superior to any other, as the writer can testify from actual experience. Mr. L. has every other description of last for making plain and fancy boots. Fifth street, between Washington and Jefferson.

CONTRACTORS AND BUILDERS.

MESSRS. WHITE & WELLER formed a partnership and commenced business as contractors and builders, February 1, 1870. They were both practical mechanics of wide experience before forming a partnershsp, and they give their personal supervision to all work entrusted to their care. They are in possession of unusual facilities for executing work in their line promptly and economically; and being enterprising and reliable, their business is rapidly on the increase.

They give special attention to the erection of dwellings, churches and school houses, and furnish plans and specifications for this class of buildings, of moderate cost, on short notice and reasonable terms.

They also make to order school furniture, and are prepared to furnish the products of others in that line, at manufacturers prices.

W. D. RICHARDSON is the contractor on the Lincoln Monument, and steadily prosecuting this beautiful work. The pavement around the capital square, which bears his name, and which he laid last year, is an evidence of his skill and genius. He is emphatically a driving business man, and his success has been well deserved and worthily earned. Mr. Richardson is prepared to take contracts for any work demanding skill, labor and money, and if a railroad to the moon was to be built, he would undertake the contract and carry it through if such a thing was possible.

CROCKERY AND GLASSWARE.

B. H. FERGUSON deals in [illegible]ry, glassware and house furnishing goods generally. His goods are partly imported and partly from American manufacturers. It is a real pleasure to visit his store. It is forty-seven by eighty-five feet. with a high ceiling and kept with the most scrupulous neatness. He sells at both wholesale and retail, the business amounting to about $40,000 annually.

There are two other crockery and glassware stores in the city.

CIGARS AND TOBACCO.

BEHNER & BIERBAUM, opposite the Postoffice, deal in Cigars, Tobaccos and Snuff. They have a large stock of these articles constantly on hand. They also deal in Confectionery, Fruits, Nuts, etc.

CONFECTIONERY AND FRUITS.

JAMES M. FITZGERALD, Manufacturer of Confectionery and Dealer in Foreign Fruits, Nuts, Wines and Fancy Groceries, west side Square. His stock of foreign fruits is at all times very large and choice, and embraces everything usually found in first class houses. Mr. Fitzgerald's establishment is one of the finest in the country, and is a credit to the city of Springfield.

CLOTHIERS AND MERCHANT TAILORS.

T. S. LITTLE has been engaged in the Clothing business in this city for about twenty-seven years, and is one of the largest dealers. In addition to a heavy stock of fine clothing and gentlemen's furnishing goods, he carries on a very extensive Merchant Tailoring establishment. Mr. Little still occupies the old stand on the South side of Capitol Square.

WOODS & HENKLE deal extensively in Clothing and Gentlemen's Furnishing Goods, and manufacture fine clothing to order. Mr. Woods has been doing business in Springfield since 1830. Mr. Henkle, for about twenty years. The present firm has been established about fifteen years. Their annual sales amount to about $60,000.

S. BENJAMIN always keeps a fine stock of g[illegible] on hand, of the latest styles, and suitable to the season. He also keeps a full line of gentlemen's furnishing goods. His sales amount to about $30,000 annually.

GEORGE A. EVANS keeps a full line of Gentlemen's Furnishing Goods, east side the Square, near the Court House.

DENTIST.

C. STODDARD SMITH is a graduate of the Philadelphia Dental College, and enjoys a good reputation as an operating Dentist. Although Dr. Smith has been in the city but a short time, he enjoys a good practice. He occupies Dr. A. W. French's old stand, just west of Bunn's Bank.

Dr. C. G. FRENCH is an old and well known practitioner in Dentistry, having been engaged in that profession for over thirty years. He avails himself of all the newest and most valuable improvements in his business, and is a skillful operator. His practice is constantly increasing, which fact establishes his character as a Dentist.

Dr. S. BABCOCK is a regular graduate of Medicine, studied Dentistry in New York, and began its practice in 1842. Since that time he has been engaged in it exclusively. Dr. Babcock came to Springfield in 1860, and has built up a first class business, which he finds increasing. The Doctor has the reputation of being a skillful Dentist, and is meeting with much success.

—11

Dr. A. W. FRENCH has been practicing for more than twenty years in Springfield. His knowledge of the profession reaches back to the time when the Dentist was only expected to replace a tooth when there were others yet remaining, to which the artificial ones could be attached by wires or silk ligatures. If all were gone his services were not called for, because he could do nothing. Then came the time for holding teeth in place by wire springs, and finally the new era was ushered in by the discovery that, when properly fitted, atmospheric pressure would hold a full set almost as firmly as the natural teeth, thus proving that

"The Dental art
Can every varying tone with ease restore,
And give thee music sweeter than before."

Dr. French is one of the best mechanical Dentists in the West, and thoroughly understands the use and comparative value of all the different kinds of material used in the art. In addition to this, he has, by his writings, done much to advance the general interests of the profession; and, as a natural consequence, has subserved the interests of all who are so unfortunate as to require the services of a Dentist.

Office on Fifth street, at the west side of Capitol Square.

Dr. ALLEN LATHAM, Dentist, Sixth street, between Adams and Monroe streets, extracts teeth without pain by aid of a galvanic battery.

Dr. F. D. LAUGHLIN is a Dental practitioner of many years' experience, and is doing a good practice in his line. He is located on Ffth street, west side of Capitol Square. He appears to thoroughly understand his profession.

DRUGGISTS.

J. B. BROWN & Co., have one of the oldest and most extensive Drug houses in Springfield. They keep on hand an extensive stock of Drugs, Medicines, Paints, Oils, and all other articles pertaining to a first class establishment. They do both a wholesale and retail business, and their sales extend over a wide territory. This house was established in 1860, and is one of the leading ones in the trade.

GLIDDEN & Co., (successors to S. H. Melvin & Co.), is one of the oldest Drug houses in Springfield, and does a large trade in Drugs, Chemicals, etc. They have one of the oldest and best stands, and sell a large amount of goods yearly. In addition to their regular Drug and Prescription business, they are extensively engaged in manufacturing fine flavoring extracts.

R. W. DILLER commenced business in the year 1849, as one of the firm of Wallace & Diller, which was the oldest established Drug store in Springfield, and has continued at the same stand ever since. The old store occupied by him was destroyed by fire in 1858, after which time he erected the building he occupies at this date.

C. E. PARKER keeps a well selected stock of Drugs, Paints, Oils, etc., together with Fancy goods and Perfumery. He attends to compounding prescriptions at all hours, in a most careful and accurate manner. Sixth street, between Monroe and Adams.

P. W. HARTS keeps Drugs and Medicines in connection with his books.—*See Book Stores.*

W. R. BEALL, Prescription Druggist corner of Fifth and Monroe streets.

DRY GOODS.

Col. JOHN WILLIAMS, of the firm of Williams & Co., is the oldest dry goods dealer in the city, having began selling goods for Major Elijah Iles in the year 1824. Col. Williams continued with Major Iles until 1830, when he purchased the establishment, and has been engaged constantly in selling goods, up to the present time. Col. Williams is known to every man, woman and child in the county, and during his long years of merchandizing he has won the good and kindly opinion of all who know him, and is to-day one of the most popular business men in the community. Col. Williams is also president of the Eirst National Bank. The firm consists of John Williams and Geo. N. Black. They deal in dry goods, groceries and Yankee notions, both wholesale and retail. Their annual sales amount to from $125,000 to $150,000.

Mr. JAMES M. GARLAND succeeds the old house of E. B. Hawley & Co., and more recenty Brinkerhoff & Garland, one oft he oldest and most favorably known establishments in Springfield. Mr. Garland was junior member of the old house, is a native of the city, and is now doing business for himself. He possesses a high reputation, and has justly won the good opinion of our citizens. The speciality of this house is, that nothing but first class goods are kept, which are marked in plain figures, at lowest cash prices. On no account, to affect sales, are goods misrepresented, and polite treatment to all customers is the invariable rule. We can, with pleasure, advise the people of this and adjoining counties to patronize this house, when desiring good articles and strictly honest dealing.

C. M. SMITH & Co. are one of the largest dry goods houses in Central Illinois. The firm is C. M. Smith & John S. Condell. Mr. Smith came, a poor boy, to Illinois in 1835, and began selling dry goods at Carrolton, Greene county, in 1837. He removed to this city in 1852, as one of the firm of Yates, Smith & Bro. Having purchased the interest of Mr. Yates, who retired, the present firm was formed in 1866. Mr. Condell began selling goods in Springfield in 1840, and was one of the well known and popular firm of Condell, Jones & Co. Mr. Smith has been in business for thirty years, has passed through all the financial troubles of the country, and has always paid one hundred cents on the dollar. The credit of this firm is unlimited, yet they buy exclusively for cash. Mr. Smith is a large property holder and identified with the interests of the city; and no man has more deservedly won advancement in business. The amount of the capital of the firm is $80,000, and their yearly business is very large.

JOHN BRESSMER is extensively engaged in the dry goods trade, at the old Tynsley corner. Mr. Bressmer has been engaged in selling goods for the last twenty-two years, in the same place he now occupies, and has been doing business by himself since 1860. He is a well known and reliable merchant, and does a large regular business. His yearly sales foot up about $60,000.

JOHN T. STUART, Jr., deals in staple and fancy dry goods, fine millinery, etc. Mr. Stuart was raised in this city, and is well known and highly appreciated by all who know him. Mr. Stuart began selling dry goods for C. M. Smith & Co., in 1857, and has been constantly engaged ever since. In 1863 he opened his present fine establishment, which is always well filled with the choicest, finest goods in his line. His sales amount to about $60,000, annually.

L. M. COLEMAN is the successor to the late firm of Brown & Coleman. This house was established three years ago, and has always enjoyed a high reputation. In Augest, last, the firm was dissolved, and Mr. Coleman purchased Major Brown's interest. He keeps a general assortment of dry goods, from the finest to the cheapest, and lace goods in endless variety. The entire second story is limited to piece goods and carpets—the stock of the latter being the finest and largest in the city. The carpet trade of this house is immense. Mr. Coleman deals strictly on an honorable, fair basis, and having permanently settled here and identified his interest with Springfield, designs to retain the large custom he has won by fair upright dealing. He employs ten clerks, carries about $60,000 worth of goods, and sells over $100,000 worth of goods, per year.

C. A. GEHRMANN, dealer in American and Foreign dry goods, ladies furs, cloaks, shawls, white goods, millinery, Paris flowers, bonnets, ribbons, etc., at wholesale and retail. West side capitol square. Business amounts to about $60,000, annually.

KIMBER & RAGSDALE keep the largest stock of foreign and domestic dry goods, of any house in the city. They erected two magnificent store rooms, which are thrown into one, on the south side of the square, at a cost of over $50,000. They certainly have the largest, finest arranged, and most elegantly furnished store in the State outside of Chicago. Mr. Kimber was, for many years, in the employ of C. M. Smith & Co., and thoroughly understands his business. They sell dry goods, carpets, boots and shoes, etc., and their sales amount to about $250,000, per year.

JOSEPH THAYER & Co. This house was established in 1835, and is therefore one of the oldest mercantile establishments in Central Illinois. This establishment is one of the reliable old places of business, for which Springfield is justly so famous. Nearly forty years, in one business in the same town, is about all the recommendation any establishment needs. Messrs. Thayer & Co. carry a very large and fine stock of goods, and sell between $75,000 and $100,000 worth per year.

DOLLAR STORES.

F. J. WILSON keeps one of the most handsome stores in the city. The variety is wonderful, and yet there is no article for which you are expected to pay more than one dollar. Everybody on visiting the city, goes to Wilson's Dollar Store, in the American House block, near the Postoffice.

O. E. DOWE, east side of the square, sells every kind of gim-crack, from a penny up to a dollar.

FEED STORE.

S. M. CULVER, wholesale and retail dealer in feed, flour, grain and country produce, grinds grain for feed, and is agent for feed mills, feed steamers and horse powers. Monroe street, near Fourth.

FURNITURE DEALERS.

J. A. HOUGH came to Springfield in 1839, and has been continuous in the furniture trade from that to the present time—thirty-two years. He is without doubt the oldest furniture dealer in Central Illinois. His sales amount to about $30,000 annually.

MR. G. WESTENBERGER buys part of his furniture in the white and finishes it in his own establishment. He employs five men in manufacturing chiefly on orders, about one-third of what he sells. His annual sales amount to about $15,-000, and his business is increasing yearly.

I. H. DAGGETT & Co., dealers in furniture, stoves, crockery, silver plated ware, and a general assoatment of house furnish ing goods, at McCreery's old stand, north side public square.

H. WILLIAMS has been in the furniture business about seventeen years, and is still carrying on business at the old stand, North Fifth street. He deals extensively in furniture of every grade, and manufactures the same to order. His purchases are made at Cincinnati, Lawrenceburg, Lafayette and Michigan, he avails himself of purchasing in the best markets. He also gives especial attention to undertaking. The sales of this house amount ta over $15,000 per year.

GROCERS.

JOHN WILLIAMS & Co., in addition to their dry goods trade, carry on an extensive grocery house, and offer for sale at wholesale and retail, a choice stock of groceries, yankee notions, etc., etc.

J. & J. W. BUNN.—This very extensive wholesale and retail grocery house was established by the senior member of the firm in 1840. This establishment was originally carried on at the corner now occupied by J. Bunn as a banking house. This long term of years makes this one of the oldest houses in this branch of mercantile business in Central Illinois. Mr. John W. Bunn has entire control of the establishment, and its successful operation fully attests his business capacity. The sales of this house amount to the very large sum of between $175,000 and $200,000 annually.

D. WICKERSHAM, dealer in provisions, and staple and fancy groceries. Mr. Wickersham has been in Springfield since 1843. He sold dry goods before the war, then commanded the Tenth Illinois cavalry four years. His place of business is at the north side of Monroe street, opposite the Post Office.

SAUNDERS & LONDON—A. H. Saunders and W. J. London. This firm deals at wholesale and retail in groceries, provisions, foreign and domestic fruits, etc., and buy and sell all kinds of country produce. The gentlemen composing this firm, are old and well known citizens and energetic men of business. Their sales amount to about $40,000, per year.

GEORGE S. CONNELLY, dealer in groceries, provisions, country produce, foreign and domestic fruits, etc., Monroe street between Fifth and Sixth. Mr. Connelly is well known in the grocery trade, having been engaged for some time past in selling goods for Capt. Floyd, and has recently gone in business for himself. He is now doing a large business.

J. G. BYERLINE, the one armed soldier, at the west side of Fifth street, between Washington, and Jefferson, deals in groceries and provisions. He is perfectly reliable, and gives you the worth of your money every time.

EDWARDS, OFFICER & Co., are among the heaviest grocery dealers in the city, and keep constantly on hand a very large stock of foreign and domestic groceries, fine fruits, flour and feed, wines, liquors and cigars. Mr. N. S. Edwards, is an old grocery merchant having been successfully engaged in that trade several years. Mr. Officer is an old and well known citizen, and Mr. J. C. Hall, has been selling groceries in this city for nearly twenty years. This firm does a business of about $70,-000 per year.

JOHN CARMODY deals in groceries and provisions, and always keeps in store a full stock of staple and fancy goods. Sales amount to about $20,000 worth annually. His store is one door south of Journal office.

WHOLESALE GROCERS.

SMITH & HAY.—This house was established by the senior member of the firm, in the year 1859. One or two changes have been made in the business, but it has steadily grown in magnitude, and been built up by the most incessant labor and unwearying energy. It is the first successful attempt to establish a strictly Wholesale Grocery house in Springfield, and its success has only been in proportion to its merits. Messrs. Smith & Hay carry, at all times, a very heavy and complete stock of goods, which they offer at lowest rates, The sales of this house amount to between four and five hundred thousand dollars annually.

HARDWARE.

W. B. MILLER keeps a very large stock, and in great variety, of all kinds of goods belonging to a first class house. Gives particular attention to all kinds of Hardware, Carriage Makers' stock, Belting, Packing, Cordage and Tackle Ropes. Mr. Miller has been in business in Springfield thirteen years. His sales average annually from $30,000 to $40,000.

SMITH & MCKINSTRY are successors to E. B. Pease, who commenced the Hardware business in Springfield in May, 1838; consequently making this the oldest established Hardware house in Central Illinois. Mr. McKinstry has been engaged in selling hardware twenty one years, ten of which have been spent in Springfield. Mr. Smith was raised in this county and has lived in Springfield since 1844. They have an elegant and well selected stock of goods, and are fully up to the times, in their line of trade.

O. F. STEBBINS has been ten years in the Hardware business in Springfield, a portion of that time being connected with the firm of Warne & Stebbins. He is now carrying on business alone and keeps every thing in his line of business, and all the latest improvements in every kind of implement. His sales average about $35,000 per year.

FOX & HOUSE deal in everything purtaining to the Hardware business. They keep on hand Wagon and Carriage materials, Blacksmith and Carpenters' tools, in great variety, and an extensive assortment of Rubber Belting. Mr. Fox has been selling hardware here for nineteen years, and is the oldest dealer now in the city.

HARNESS AND SADDLES.

J. O. RAMES, harness and saddle manufacturer, and dealer in saddles, harness, whips, wool collars, bridles and every other article in the line of his business. Fifth street south of Bunn's Bank.

BUSHER, WYATT & Co. are wholesale and retail dealers in leather and saddlery hardware, saddles, bridles, collars, whips, belting, etc., etc. They manufacture very extensively, and make the greater portion of the harness they sell. Mr Busher, the senior member of the firm came to Springfield in 1836, and commenced the tanning, and currying business on a very extensive scale, but soon found he was years in advance of the demands of the country. Since that time he has been very extensively engaged in manufacturing and selling saddles, harness, etc., etc. This firm carries a large stock, and sells about $50,-000, worth per year.

R. J. COATS, dealer in and manufacturer, of fine buggy and coach harness, leather and saddlery hardware. Corner Washington, and seventh streets.

Leland Hotel.

ably enlarged and much improved since that time. It is easy of access, being but one square from the depot of the Chicago and St. Louis railroad, and yet, is sufficiently retired to afford all the attractions of a home to a weary traveler. It affords accommodations for about one hundred and fifty guests, and is first class in all its appointments. John McCreery, Proprietor.

THE CHENERY HOUSE is one of the oldest and best known hotels in the city. The present proprietors, W. D. Chenery & Son, purchased the house of Joel Johnson, Esq., in October, 1855. Since that time they expended in additions to the property, over $20,000. The Chenery enjoys a high reputation, and among the many excellent hotels at the capital, ranks No. 1. Messrs. John W. and James Chenery have charge of the office. This house accommodates about two hundred guests.

THE WESTERN HOTEL is situated at the corner of Third and Jefferson street, opposite the Chicago and Alton depot. This house was built in 1868, and being new, everything is in good condition, neat and clean. This house is built in modern style and possesses all the conveniences of a first-class hotel. It is kept by the owner, John Shoeneman, Esq.

Besides the above hotels, Springfield has the American, Everett and Revere, first-class houses, making a total of seven hotels, offering the best accommodaiions for about fifteen hundred persons, besides a number of smaller hotels and boarding houses.

HOTELS.

THE LELAND HOTEL would be considered one of the finest hotels, if it was in New York City, Boston or Philadelphia, and has no superior in tha Western States. There is no State capital in the Union that can boast of a finer house. It is justly the pride of the citizens of Springfield, and universally admired by all who visit the capital. To say that it is first-class does not do it justice, for it is much more. It was built by a joint stock company in 1866, and opened to the public January 1, 1867, by Horace S. Leland, Esq., the present proprietor. To say that it is kept by a Leland is a sufficient guarantee that it is all that could be desired by the most fastidious epicure.

This is one of the chain of hotels kept by the Lelands, beginning with the St. Charles Hotel—European plan—New York City, Delavan House, Albany, N. Y.; Clarendon Hotel, Saratoga Springs, N. Y.; and Grand Union Hotel, Saratoga Springs, N. Y.

Capt. Wiggins, an experienced and justly popular hotel man, has immediate charge of the house, and under his superintendence everything is conducted in the finest and best of style.

ST. NICHOLAS HOTEL.—This fine house was built in 1856, and has been consider-

LAMPS AND LAMP GOODS.

JOSEPH LEFEVRE & Co. are new men in the city. They make a specialty of a single article for lighting stores, dwellings etc. It is called Danforth's Petroleum Fluid, a new article prepared from petroleum oil. From a great number of tests it underwent in my presence I *know* that it is absolutely *non-explosive.* It gives such a clear steady light as to make it far preferable to the best gas light.

Messrs Lefevre & Co. deal in all styles of lamps and lamp goods. Their store is on Adams street, near the town clock.

HATS, CAPS AND FURS.

FRED DIENES, deals in hats, caps, gloves, furs, and repairs furs. opposite Bradford's book store, Sixth street, near the Post office.

J. H. ADAMS, dealer in hats, caps, furs, etc., all of the latest styles. He is the oldest dealer in this line in the city. Store, west side of Capitol Square.

C. WOLF & Co. deal in hats, caps, and fine fur goods. They keep a large stock of these goods on hand, together with a choice stock of gentlemen's furnishing goods.

LIQUOR DEALERS.

G. A. MAYER, wholesale dealer in imported wines, liquors, champagnes, California wines, brandies and Kentucky whiskeys. Monroe street, between Fifth and Sixth.

THOMAS BRADY has been engaged in business in Springfield since 1853. For the last fifteen years he has devoted his attention exclusively to the wholesale liquor trade, and has built up a very extensive business. He deals in fine wines, liquors and everything pertaining to this branch of business. Adams street, south side of the square.

H. E. MUELLER, importer and wholesale dealer in all kinds of liquors. His place of business is at the Opera House.

J. B. FOSSELMAN came to Springfield in 1850, was six years in the drug business and eleven years in the grocery trade, wholesale and retail. He was the first, or among the first, to send out traveling agents to solicit business, to build up wholesale trade in Springfield, and in war times found the business very successful. He is now in the wholesale liquor trade on Fifth street, north of the square.

LUMBER YARDS.

SCHUCK & BAKER deal in pine, poplar, ash, oak and wagon lumber, and in sash, doors, blinds and all other materials used in building. Their sales amount to about $80,000 annually. Their yard is near the depot of the T. W. & W. railroad.

VREDENBURG & EILSON sell lumber to the value of about $65,000 annually.

J. S. VREDENBURG is the oldest lumber merchant in the city, having been in the trade about sixteen years. His annual sales are about $90,000. His lumber yard is near the C. A. & St. L. railroad depot.

E. S. JOHNSON also has a yard near the same depot, making four establishments whose annual sales foot up between $250,000 and $300,000.

MARBLE YARDS.

JOSEPH BAUM is properly a sculptor, having served a regular apprenticeship in the ancient city of Cologne. He was in South Carolina when the rebellion broke out and lost nearly all his property. His yard is at the corner of Jefferson and Fourth streets, where he is prepared to do all kinds of Marble and Stone cutting.

ADAM JOHNSON is an old dealer in Marble. His sales for the last five years have been about $18,000 annually.

MUSIC AND MUSICAL INSTRUMENTS.

G. W. CHATTERTON keeps a fine assortment of Pianos from the most celebrated manufacturers; also, other kinds of Musical Instruments and Music. He keeps his musical instruments in connection with his fine stock of Watches and Jewelry; which see.

J. M. PEARSON is one of our oldest dealers in Music and Musical Instruments, He has recently removed into new quarters, where he always has on hand a full supply of Bradbury's Pianos, Organs and other Musical instruments. He also has for sale H. Knauff & Son's Church Organs, which are universally conceded to be the very best instruments of their kind. They are selected with much care, and parties desiring a truly first class instrument can always be accommodated.

Mr. Pearson makes a specialty of keeping imported Music, and always has the latest and choicest. He has, at all times, the latest publications of J. Schuferth & Co., and all other late and fashionable music for the Piano. This department is very full at all times, and all the musical gems can here be found.

Mr. WILLIAM PEARSON occupies the same building. He deals very extensively in fine Pictures and Picture Frames, and has for sale some of the choicest works of art. A visit to, and examination of, his establishment, will amply repay any one possessing a love of the beautiful in art, and an appreciation of that which is refined and elegant. The citizens of Springfield should take pride in supporting and encouraging this establishment, which is not only a source of much credit to the proprietor, but is an ornament to the city. All the latest gems of art will be found at Mr. Pearson's, and it will afford him pleasure at all times to show visitors through his establishment.

DEWITT'S TEMPLE OF MUSIC.—This establishment is in the fourth year of its existence, and has met with success unknown heretofore. Mr. J. A. DeWitt, the proprietor, is one of our enterprising citizens. Determined to make his house the great depot for Music and Musical instruments, he has succeeded; and his establishmet is now the resort of all lovers of music and those in want of musical instruments. Mr. DeWitt is agent for the matchless "Steinway," and keeps a full line of the Mathushek, Orchestral, and Colibri, Haines Bro's., and other Pianos, and a great variety of Organs; among others, the Mason & Hamlin, DeWitt Bros., Eureka Grand, Needham & Son, etc. These instruments are rented or sold on monthly payments. About six months since Mr. DeWitt commenced publishing sheet music. Many of his pieces have attained great popularity, among others, "Come to me, darling," by Prof. Meissner, and "We have parted," by Lam. French. "Sleep, sister, sleep," by J. A. DeWitt, in reply to "Put me in my little bed," bids fair to be as popular as the song to which it responds. "Take me but spare my boy," by S. W. Belcher, and "Dear mother, do not die," by Lam. French, are fresh from the press. They are touchingly beautiful and much admired. Mr. DeWitt receives in exchange for his publications, all the new music as soon as issued. This enables him to fill orders by mail from all parts of the country. Persons at a distance can get what they want at reasonable prices by sending to his "Temple of Music." Mr. DeWitt's motto is, "Large sales and small profits." He does not claim to sell goods *at or below cost*, but claims a small profit on each sale. Persons visiting the "Temple of Music" will always find gentlemanly attendants, who will take great pleasure in showing them around.

NEWSPAPERS.

Prepared by HARRY C. WATSON.

THE ILLINOIS STATE JOURNAL.

This paper is the oldest in the State of Illinois. The Sangamo *Spectator*, was first issued by Hooper Warren in 1826- and was succeded by and merged into the Sangamo Journal, which was published by Simeon and Josiah Francis Esqs. On December 11th. 1839, a semi-weekly was issued. On the 23rd. of September 1847, the title was changed to Illinois Journal. On the 13th. of June 1848, the first daily was issued.

In July 1855, Mr. Bailhache and E.L. Baker Esqs. purchased the establishment and S. Francis retired. On the 15th. of December 1863, the *Illinois State Journal* company, was organized and chartered. On the 25th. of August 1863,

Mr. H. Bailhache retired, and was succeded by D. L. Phillips Esq. The present officers of the company are E. L. Baker, President; D. L. Phillips, Vice President; and J. D. Roper, Secretary. Mr. Roper is also the very efficient and thorough going cashier of the institution. The company consists of E. L. Baker, D. L. Phillips, John P. Baker and J. M. Culbertson Esq. The Journal is the official state paper, is firm and consistent, republican in politics and is a very influential and live newspaper. E. L. Baker, and J. M. Culbertson are the political editors, Col. John P. Baker, General news and L. M. Snell Esq. city editor.

The *Journal* book and job office is one of the finest in the State, and in the entire appointments and completeness, has but few equals. A large sterotype department is connected therewith, the whole being under the direction of first class and efficient workmen. The *Journal* is the state organ of the republican party, and ably fills that position. The terms are Daily $10, per year. Tri-Weekly $6. Weekly $2.

ILLINOIS STATE REGISTER.

The Illinois State *Register* newspaper office was removed from Vandalia (then the State capital) to Springfield, in 1836, shortly after the paper was first started. Its proprietors, Messrs. Walters & Weber, were State printers. On January 2, 1849, the first daily *Register* was issued by Charles H. Lanphier and Geo. Walker, Esqs., who had succeeded Walters & Weber. In January, 1858, Mr. Walker dissolved his connection with the paper, and was succeeded by E. L. Conner, who purchased his share. In June, 1860, Mr. Lanphier purchased Mr. Conner's interest and assumed entire control of the paper. In the fall of 1863 a stock company purchased the office, and under its management the *Register* was conducted until January 1, 1865, when E. L. & J. D. Merritt, the present proprietors, purchased the office. The *Register* has for many years been recognized throughout the State as the State organ of the Democratic party of Illinois. It has a wide circulation and influence, and is in a prosperous condition. Judge J. W. Merritt, and E. L. Merritt, Esq., are editors, and Major Louis Souther, city editor. A first-class book and job office is connected with the establishment. The *Register* is furnished at $10 per year for the Daily, and $2 for the Weekly.

—12

THE MASONIC TROWEL.

Harman G. Reynolds, the editor and present publisher of the *Trowel*, is one of the oldest masons in the State, having taken his degrees in Warsaw Lodge, in 1843. He was Grand Marshal of the Grand Lodge in 1848, and was elected Grand Secretary of the Grand Lodge and Chapter, and continued as Grand Secretary of the Lodge until 1851. In 1868 he was elected Grand Master, and held this position for two years. He remained Secretary of the Grand Chapter until 1869. He assisted in the initiatory work of forming the Grand Council of Royal and Select Masters, and was the first Recorder of that body. Mr. Reynolds has been Master of three Lodges and High Priest of three Chapters, and was first Commander of Elwood Commandery No. 6, of this city. All of which positions he filled with credit to himself and honor to the fraternity. He also received, in Chicago, in 1854, the thirty-second degree of the Ancient Scottish Rites, and the thirty-third in Boston, in 1864. In 1858, he located in this city, and established in 1862 the *Masonic Trowel*, with which paper he retained his connection until 1868. He has always had the editorial control of its columns, and his labors therein have redounded to the general welfare and prosperity of the craft at large. By the fire on the night of the 22d of February, by which the *Trowel* was destroyed, he was stripped of every dollar of his earthly possessions. But true to his nature, he rises superior to adverse fortune, and is once more hard at work. He has always been a live, working man, and now his numerous friends should see that he receives some substantial proof of their appreciation. He designs continuing the publication of the *Trowel*, and he certainly, after a long life spent in the work, is entitled to the kindly consideration of the bretheren of "the mystic tie."

THE ILLINOIS ATLAS

Is a nine column weekly paper, and is published by the Illinois Atlas Company. It is independent in all things, neutral in nothing, and is a live, wide-awake readable sheet. The circulation of the *Atlas* is very large, and is constantly being extended. D. J. Snow, Esq., a well known editor, now has charge of the editorial department, and will in future devote his entire attention to the *Atlas*. The terms for subscription are $1 50 per year in advance.

ILLINOIS STAATS DEMOKRAT.

After several decidedly unsuccessful attempts to establish a German paper in Springfield, in the spring of 1866, Mr. C. Lohman established the *Illinois Staats Demokrat*, and since that time has carried the paper on successfully. The *Demokrat*, as its title denotes, advocates Democratic principles, and enjoys an extensive circulation in the city and throughout Central Illinois, and is very popular as a local newspaper among the Germans in this section of the State. Mr. Lohman is a practical printer. The interests of Springfield are well represented among the Germans by this large and well conducted paper.

THE CENTRAL ILLINOIS ZEITUNG.

This new candidate for public favor is puplished by the Central Illinois Zeitung Company, Prof. VonElsner, editor. The *Zeitung* is devoted to Republicanism, and promises to be an influentual sheet. It is published weekly, and already has secured a large circulation in the city and vicinity.

PRINTING OFFICES.

Mr. John H. Johnson now has entire charge of the Job Printing Office formerly belonging to the late firm of Johnson & Bradford, on the west side of the Capitol Square. This office is well stocked and in complete running order. Mr. Johnson is prepared to do all kinds of plain and fine book and job printing, in the best manner. A large bindery is also connected with this establishment.

B. A. Richards & Co.—This firm is composed of Ben. A. Richards, who has been engaged in the printing business in this city for nearly twenty-five years, and Frank Hudson, jr., who is also well known to our citizens. Their office is on North Sixth street, and is one of the finest in the city. They devote their time exclusively to fine job printing, and the work turned out by them is not excelled in the State of Illinois.

George R. Weber, Esq., one of the oldest printers in this section of the country, has a very good and complete job office on North Sixth street, between Washington and Jefferson streets. This office is well prepared to do all kinds of job work.

Britt & Cassett.—Thomas J. Britt and L. Cassett, two well known and popular Printers, are now carrying on the job printing office on the west side of North Sixth street, between Jefferson and Washington streets. They have all the late improvements in the printing art, and their presses, type and materials generally, are first class.

NOTIONS AND TOYS.

Smith & Bro. keep an extensive stock of notions, and fancy goods, and transact almost an exclusive wholesele business. They keep every article in their line, known to the trade.

Their store, at the north side of the square, is one hundred and fifty feet deep, and their facilities, for the transaction of business, are unsurpassed. They have been eight years in the business, with a growing trade, and offer every advantage that can be given by any house in the west.

PAINTERS, PAINTS, PAPER HANGERS AND DEALERS IN WALL PAPER.

THOMAS & HART, do all kinds of house, sign and decorative painting and paper hanging. Their imitations of Sienna, Egyptian green, Italian pink, Verde antique, and all other kinds of marble, would lead the unpracticed eye to think they were genuine articles.

Of woods, their imitations are so perfect, that it would seem superfluous for nature to furnish more than one or two kinds, then Thomas & Hart would supply from these, the oak, walnut, maple mahogany, Satin wood, and all other kinds. Their paintings in imitation of the different kinds of wood, have taken the premium in the State fairs, at Quincy and Chicago. Their fresco paintings, are universally admired, also their wall paintings in imitations of silk, diaper, embossed leather, damask and morocco.

These gentlemen thoroughly understand their business, and are ambitious that none shall excel them, in the beauty and accuracy of their work. Monroe street between Fourth and Fifth.

MAJ. N. H. ALDEN, deals in paints, oils, varnishes, glass, and painters supplies in all varieties. He also deals in wall papers, borders, window shades, curtain fixtures, etc., etc. a fine variety of which will always be found upon his counters. He also does to order painting, graining and paper hanging, and has a competant *corps* of assistants, in those departments.

His place of business is on Monroe street between Fourth and Fifth streets,

JOSEPH RUCKEL, is one of the old established business men, having been doing business for over twenty years. During the great fire, which occured on the night of the 22nd. of February, Mr. Ruckel's store was burned down. Since then he has removed on the opposite side of Fifth between Monroe and Adams, and has opened an entire new stock. It embraces wall paper, window shades, curtains, and curtain fixtures, a most extensive variety of which will always be found on hand.

R. B. ZIMMERMAN, came to Springfield in 1835, and has been in his present business since 1839, this for an old settled country would not be remarkable, but thirty-two years continuously in one business, is a long time for so new a country.

R. R. PAYRAN, is a carriage painter, and does trimming, and general repairing in that line of business.

PHOTOGRAPHERS.

C. S. GERMAN has been engaged in Photographing in Springfield over ten years, is the oldest in the city, and is a successful operator, as his large business most conclusively proves. His work has always been of a high order, and compares favorably with that of any gallery in the west. He pays particular attention to getting up fine work, large and small copying and coloring. If you want a good looking picture you must take a good looking countenance with you, as he will surely show you just as you look. State Gallery, west side of the square.

M. DUBOCE takes pictures in every style of the art of photography, and gives particular attention to ambrotype gems. He has among his specimens some beautiful views of the new State capitol, and other objects of interest around the city. Gallery on Sixth street, between Monroe and Adams. He has also for sale some beautiful stereoscopic views of Oak Ridge and many prominent buildings in the city.

FRED P. MOBSBY is known as a skillful artist, and has been most fortunate in pleasing the tastes and wishes of all desiring fine pictures. His work fully attests his skill, and speaks for itself. He is constantly adding new improvements to his appliances, and is prepared to execute work to the entire satisfaction of all. Gallery west side of the square.

I. H. VOORHIS, of the National Gallery, is well known as a popular artist, having been engaged here for several years. Everything in his line, photographs, gems, etc., are taken "true to nature," at his gallery. Mr. Voorhis avails himself of all the latest and most useful improvements in his art, and is thoroughly posted therein. He sends out nothing but first-class work.

PHYSICIANS.

Charles Ryan,	S. Townsend,
H. Wohlgemuth,	A. Trapp,
Wm. Jayne,	W. H. Davis,
J. W. Dresser,	A. L. Converse,
B. M. Griffith,	Wm. Place,
N. Wright,	C. H. Lane,
H. B. Buck,	E. A. Artsman,
George T. Allen,	F. Keuchler,
R. S. Lord,	G. W. Morgan,
H. C. Barrell,	H. N, Keener,
B. Fox,	J. A. Vincent,
J. L. Million,	W. B. Condell.
T. S. Henning,	

OCCULISTS.

J. D. Harper, H. H. Roman.

DR. H. WOHLGEMUTH.—Among the old citizens of Springfield we may be allowed to say a few words with reference to this gentleman, who has practised in this city longer than any other man now engaged in the duties of his profession. Dr. Wohlgemuth left his native country, Hanover, Germany, in 1845, and came to Springfield in the same year. He commenced the practice of medicine here in 1846, and labored under many disadvantages at first, but his life has been very successful. At the time he came to Springfield there were thirteen other practicing physicians here. Of this number ther is but one residing in the city—Dr. P. Moran, who long since retired from practice on account of old age and failing health. Drs. Hughes, Merriman, Cabines, Lustar, Henry, Richardson, Wallace, Todd, Gersham Jayne, Huggins, M. Helm, and others, have passed away from their earthly labors since his arrival.

It is not in his profession only, that Dr. Wohlgemuth has made his influence felt, but he has in many ways become identified with the growth and prosperity of the city of his adoption. He has in an eminent degree enjoyed the confidence of his patrons as a practitioner of medicine; and as a public spirited citizen, has received evidences of confidence and esteem. He has at various times discharged the duties of City Physician, and County Physician, Director of Public Schools, and Member of the City Council.

Much credit is due to him, as Manager of Oak Ridge Cemetery, in which capacity he served for a number of years. He with his co-laborers, took charge of those grounds, when all was covered with a thick growth of underbrush, which could hardly be realized by those who have seen it only in its present high state of culture, and ornamentation.

The most important acts of the public life of Dr. Wohlgemuth, has been his labor, in connection with Col. John Williams and C. W. Matheny, Esq., as Commissioners for the construction of the City Water Works of Springfield. This work required two years of unremitting exertion on their part, and was completed to the entire satisfaction of the public.

As the Doctor is now only about fifty years of age, he is still active in his profession, with a store of experience, which will be of much value to his patrons for years to come.

SPRINGFIELD INFIRMARY AND PRIVATE HOSPITAL.—DR. WILLIAM H. DAVIS is the proprietor of this establishment. Besides an extensive city practice he makes a specialty of surgery and treatment of cases of chronic diseases. Here the patient, suffering from any lingering malady, requiring the constant care of a skillful physician, can enjoy all the comforts of a home and careful nursing, at the same time.

The reputation of Dr. Davis for the kind and watchful care over his patients, and his skill in treating these ailments, is so well established, that those who are in need of such treatment should not hesitate a moment in placing themselves under his care.

The infirmary is on Washington street, near the depot of the Chicago and St. Louis Railroad.

DR. J. D. HARPER came to Springfield in 1853, and entered upon the practice of his profession. From that to the present time he has made diseases of the eye and ear a specialty. From personal knowledge, I have reason to believe that making the treatment of these delicate organs a constant study, has been a blessing to many thus afflicted.

The foregoing list comprises the names of the leading medical men of Springfield. It embraces some of the principal practioners in the profession, of whom some very interesting biographical sketches might be added.

PORK PACKING.

MR. JAMES LAMB came to Springfield in the year 1831, and has been actively engaged in business during all the intervening years. He commenced packing pork in 1834–35, and has continued it to the present time. Springfield has been his home during all that time; but, in order to save the expense of transportation, before railroads came into use, he for a few years did his packing first at Kaskaskia, next at Alton, and then at Beardstown. Since 1842 his operations have been confined to Springfield. For the last fifteen years his transactions have been very large, paying out, annually, from two hundred and fifty to three hundred thousand dollars, reaching the highest point in 1864, which amounted to half a million dollars. He has one of the finest, most substantial, and best arranged buildings for pork packing in the Western country.

Mr. Lamb has been, at different times, engaged in manufacturing, and has always been among the foremost citizens to encourage enterprises calculated to develop the resources of the country and build up trade. Every movement for the religious, mental and moral elevation of those around him, has always found in him a liberal supporter.

SEWING MACHINES.

J. H. H. BENNET sells the Singer Sewing Machine, and by his fair dealing, prompt attention to the wants of his customers, and complete mastery of this favorite machine, has merited and won the confidence of his patrons.

During the year 1870 the Singer Manufacturing Co. sold 127,625 machines—44,625 more than were sold by any other company. Of these sales Mr. Bennett made his full proportion.

ADAM M. STEIN is agent for the American Button Hole Over-seaming Sewing Machine, which possesses two peculiarities, which are expressed by its name. It has an attachment for cutting and working button holes, and another device for overseaming, besides doing all other kinds of family sewing. This is one of the best machines in use. His place of business is on South Fifth street.

HUNT & YOUNG carry on the State office of the Howe Sewing Machine Company. They began business about one year ago, and since that time have disposed of 1300 machines. Their business last year foots up nearly $80,000, and they expect the coming year to nearly double that amount. Over 90,000 machines a year are manufactured and sold by the company, which is a proof of their merits. Messrs. Hunt & Young have finely fitted sales rooms, and are prepared to promptly fill all orders at No. 9, Monroe street.

STOVES AND TINWARE.

MR. E. KREIGH deals in cook and heating stoves, furnaces and house furnishing goods. He also manufactures all kinds of tin, copper and sheet iron ware. His store is on Fifth street, between Adams and Monroe. Mr. Kreigh is one of the oldest and most respected citizens and business men of Springfield.

Geo. W. Bolinger deals in stoves, tin ware, crockery and house furnishing goods generally. He also puts up gutters, spouts and metal roofing.

Robinson & Bauman, dealers in stoves, and manufacturers of tin, sheet iron, and copper.

They are also agents for marbleized iron, mantel, and grates, hot air furnaces, and patent tile. Their sales amount to about $25,000, annually. Store and shop, on Fifth street, north of the First National Bank.

Henry Bugg, is manufacturer of and dealer in stoves, tin, and sheet iron ware. He also sells pumps, and deals in queens ware. North side of Capitol Square.

C. H. Edmands, deals in stoves, tin, and sheet iron ware, and puts up roofing and guttering. Gives particular attention to street and saloon lanterns, lamps, and lamp posts. Monroe street, between Fifth and Sixth.

L. F. Dyson, deals in stoves, tin and hollow ware, wooden ware, etc. He also does roofing and guttering. His annual sales are about $15,000. His place of business is on Washington street, east of the Court House.

H. C. Cullom, wholesale and retail dealer in stoves and tin ware, and agricultural implements. Manufacturer of tin, copper, sheet iron, and zinc work. He gives particular attention to steam mill, and railroad work. Does roofing, guttering, and spouting to order. Store on Monroe street opposite the Post Office.

WATCHES, CLOCKS AND JEWELRY.

W. D. Ward deals in watches from the best manufactories, both in Europe and America, but he gives particular attention to the Waltham and Elgin watches, and will keep those of the Springfield Watch Company, as soon as they are in the market.

Of clocks, he keeps all the best kinds, and will supply, to order, any kind that may be called for, if it is to be obtained. Silver Ware from the manufactory of Rogers & Brothers, Meriden, Conn., he always keeps a full assortment of.

The American Spectacle Company, of Detroit, Mich., is well represented in Mr. Ward's show cases. These Spectacles are made from the Brazilian rock quartz, without any heat whatever. The pebble is taken in its natural condition, sawed into thin plates and then polished. These glasses are said to be superior to any other substance known for preserving the eye. West side of Fifth street opposite the Square.

A. H. Fisher deals extensively in fine jewelry of every description, selected with much care from the largest houses in the East. His stock comprises every thing usually found in first class establishments, including all the rich and novel styles of fashionable jewelry and silver ware. He pays particular attention to regulating and repairing fine watches, and has the best of workmen in his employ. His establishment is in Keuchler's fine building, opposite the Postoffice.

George W. Chatterton has been established at the stand he now occupies on the west side of the square, since 1839, and is consequently one of the oldest, if not the oldest, established Jeweler in Central Illinois. Mr. Chatterton, in addition to his varied stock of fine jewelry, has always kept a large and fine stock of Pianos, musical instruments and musical merchandise. The stock is very large, full and complete, and embraces everything usually found in a first class establishment of this character. Mr. Chatterton is a practical watch, clock and chronometer maker, and has devoted many years to repairing the same. All orders from abroad will receive his especial attention, and be filled with entire satisfaction to his patrons.

DEALERS IN WOOD, COAL AND BALED HAY.

Hobert T. Ives has been in other business in Springfield since 1859, but commenced the present business in 1870.

FLOURING MILLS, BREWERIES GRAIN ELEVATORS AND THE GRAIN TRADE.

The grain trade and its manufacture, partaking as it does of the characteristics of both mercantile and manufacturing, I have grouped all the business relating to either branch, together, here between the two.

FLOURING MILLS.

M. Hickox is the proprietor of the Excelsior Mills. They have three run of burrs, and are capable of making about 150 barrels of flour every twenty-four hours- Mr. Hickox pays the highest cash price for wheat, and transacts business to the amount of about $50,000 annually.

Wackerle & Rapps are the proprietors of the Phoenix Mills. The mills have capacity to make about 125 barrels of flour daily. Their sales amount to about $40,000 annually.

Logan & Ridgely are the proprietors of Everybody's Mill. Do a large amount of custom work, and buy wheat also. The capacity of the mill is from 125 to 150 barrels per day.

William McCague is proprietor of the Ætna Mills. They have three run of burrs, and are capable of making about 150 barrels of flour every twenty-four hours. He buys wheat at all times, and his annual sales amount to from $50,000 to $60,000 annually.

B. F. Haines & Co. are the proprietors of the Illinois Mills. This establishment was built in the year 1861, with four run of burrs, and is capable of making about 200 barrels of flour in twenty-four hours. This is the largest mill in the city, but none of them are worked to their full capacity. The sales of B. F. Haines & Co. run from $70,000 to $80,000 annually. Mr. Addison Hickox, the partner of Mr. Haines, is the oldest miller, and has built more mills, than any other man in Sangamon county.

BREWERIES.

F. Reisch & Son are the oldest brewers in the city, having been carrying on the business here for over twenty years. Two years ago they spent over fifty thousand dollars in additions to their brewery and now have one of the finest and most complete establishments in the State. They employ sixteen hands, purchase and use 30,000 bushels of barley per year, and do a business of $100,000 per annum. The value of their buildings, etc., is $100,000.

Fischer & Co. are successors to M. K. Keydell. Their fine brewery is situated in the northwest portion of the city, and Keydell's Park is known as one of the most beautiful spots in Springfield. This firm employs twelve men, buys about fifteen thousand bushels of barley per year, and sell about $60,000 worth per year. The value of the brewery and grounds is over $75,000.

John Landheimer has a brewery in operation in the south-west part of the city. He does a small business, however, only for home consumption.

Nolte & Ackerman carry on an extensive brewery in the west part of the city. It was built by Phillip Ackerman in 1864. In 1869 Mr. A. Nolte, a well known business man became associated with Mr. Ackerman, and has with him built up a large business. This firm makes and sells about four thousand barrels of beer per year, and employ six hands in its manufacture.

GRAIN AND GRAIN ELEVATOR.

Messrs. Post & Eastman commenced building a grain elevator, near the depot of the Chicago and St. Louis Railroad, in the spring of 1865, and completed it in January, 1866. It is sixty feet wide, seventy feet long, and one hundred and ten feet high. The first seventy-five feet from the ground is iron clad, as a protection against fire. The whole building is erected in the most solid and substantial manner, and cost $62,000. The elevator is constructed with bins capable of holding 120,000 bushels of grain. In addition to this there are corn cribs belonging to the proprietors, and on the same lots, with capacity for about 30,000 bushels. A steam engine runs the hoisting machinery, and with everything in order they can receive and ship from eight to ten thousand bushels of grain, per day. The elevator firm receives and ships about one quarter of a million bushels of wheat annually. The five mills buy and manufacture an average of 50,000 bushels each, besides one or two outside parties, who buy and ship on a small scale, making a total of about half a million bushels of wheat received at this market, annually. The quantity of corn and oats received here amounts, in the aggregate, to about half a million bushels also. About 75,000 bushels of barley are used in the breweries in Springfield, and in addition to this the grain dealers buy and ship barley also. The total quantity of grain of all kinds received at the Springfield market, is about one and a quarter millions of bushels annually.

The elevator is now owned by Eastman & Co.—Col. John Williams having taken the place of Mr. Post October 10, 1870.

MANUFACTURING ESTABLISHMENTS.

All of the ten or twelve stove and tin ware dealers in the city have more or less work done in tin, copper and sheet iron; but none of them are entitled to the dignity of being called a manufactory, because there is not a stove foundery in the place.

There is a considerable number of men engaged in making boots and shoes, but each man has his own kit of tools, which he could pack and march at a minute's notice; there is consequently nothing like a manufactory in this line of business.

Of all the eight or ten furniture dealers, the principal portion of them have some work made about their places of business; but as there is no machinery used, and no propelling power except human muscles, the only appropriate language is to say, there is no furniture factory in the city.

I might go over a great many more branches of business, in detail, with the same result; but the best way to show what the vacancies are and what there is not, is to show what there is. The following firms and companies comprise all there is in the way of manufactories in Springfield.

BOILER MAKERS.

Wilson & Drake have a boiler shop, here and at Decatur. Mr. Drake resides here, and has been running this shop for six years. They do repairing of all kinds and make boilers to order.

CARRIAGE AND WAGON MANUFACTORY.

A. Booth, Son & Co. The senior member of this firm commenced business about seven miles north of Springfield, in the year 1840. In 1854 he removed his establishment to Springfield, where the business has increased steadily to the present time. They now make about 800 vehicles per year. Their work is chiefly on road wagons, but they make a considerable number of carriages and buggies. They give employment to twenty-five hands, and their annual sales amount to about $75,000.

Their business is now growing faster than at any previous era of this history. In order to meet the demands of the trade they are erecting a mammoth store house, for sales rooms, at the corner of Adams and Eighth street, one square south of their factory.

McDonald & Bro. commenced, January 1, 1868, the manufacture of carriages, buggies and spring wagons. They employ from ten to twenty men. Manufacture all the time, and do repairing when called for. They use none but the best of materials, and employ the best workmen to be obtained in the country. Business amounts to from $15,000 to $20,000 annually. Messrs. McDonald & Bro. are both young and energetic, and bid fair to build up a fine business.

Withey Brothers, three in number, commenced business in Springfield in 1854, and, by industry and perseverance, have built up a fine trade. After six years incessant labor their shops were almost totally destroyed by a hurricane, August 6, 1860. They immediately rebuilt, and on the 19th of April, 1861, their factory was swept away by fire. With undaunted courage they have toiled on, and now have a fine establishment, giving employment to about twenty-five men. They make principally fine carriages and buggies, and some lumber wagons. Their sales average from $50,000 to $60,000, annually.

Myers & Talbott make some new work, and do a general repairing business. Employ seven men, and do a business of about $12,000 annually.

Mr. August Kessberger commenced building wagons in Springfield in the year 1861. He was without capital, and

increased his business only as his earnings would justify it. Mr. Kessberger is the inventor and patentee of what is called the Iron Clad Pipe Axle. It is a combination of wrought iron pipe, with cast iron skeins or axles arms, with wood filling, and has a truss rod beneath, for making the axle more firm. The patent includes an attachment for a ring bolt, without making a hole through the axle and bolster, thus retaining all the strength at every point. This axle is undoubtedly a valuable invention, and wagon manufacturers elsewhere would do well to consult Mr. Kessberger, who has rights for the use of the patent for sale, either for shops, counties or States.

Mr. K. has recently formed a partnership with several of his workmen, and the style of the firm is A. Kessberger & Co. Thirteen men find employment here, and manufacture about 200 wagons annually, amounting to about $20,000.

Allen Miller has been about fourteen years making carriages and wagons in Springfield. His principal business is building fine buggies and carriages, and doing general repairing. He works from six to ten men. Shops on Monroe street near the city hall.

Jacob Divelbiss commenced making wagons in Springfield in the year 1837, and continued in business until 1868, when he was succeeded by Beard & Hodge. In February, 1870, Mr. Beard withdrew from the firm.

Mr. Jacob Hodge is now the sole proprietor, and he works an average of six hands, making lumber wagons, spring wagons, and does general repairing. This establishment has, for thirty-four years, sustained its reputation for good work, and it is not likely to degenerate in the hands of the present proprietor. Shops on North Eighth street.

FOUNDRIES AND MACHINE SHOPS.

The Ætna Foundry, and Machine Shops, were established by Lowry, Lamb, & Co. in 1848. The present shops were erected in 1849. At one time woolen machinery was in operation, in a part of the building, and at another two or three thousand plows were made annually. The business now is confined, principally to foundry work, and building steam engines, and mill machinery. From twenty-five to thirty-five hands are employed, and the business transacted amounts to about $50,000, annually. Mr. John C. Lamb is the present proprietor.

TOLEDO, WABASH & WESTERN Railway Shops. The company employs about 310 men, who receive their pay, at this point, and the monthly pay roll is about $20,000. Of this number about 180, are employed in the shops, under monthly pay, of between $12,000, and $13,000. —*See article on T. W. & W. Railway, page* 33.

S. F. EASTMAN, keeps a shop for repairing all kinds of farm and mill machinery. Works four men, and runs a steam engine of eight horse power.

The EXCELSIOR FOUNDRY, and Machine works, were established in 1854, and have been in the hands of the present proprietors, Messrs. Berryman & Ripon, since 1856. They are both practical workmen, and have the reputation of understanding their business thoroughly.

As an evidence of the estimation, in which their work is held at home, I need only refer to the fact that the steam engines and hoisting apparatus for all the four coal shafts in this county, were made at this establishment. They not only give special attention to coal mining machinery, but do all kinds of mill work, and every thing else pertaining to a first class establishment of the kind.

This firm employs from twenty-five to forty men and do a business amounting to about $50,000, annually.

The Alexander Corn Planter, Factory, has a foundry for doing its own work, but no other.

KING'S SAUCE ROYAL.

In the fall of 1869 William King commenced manufacturing a condiment for the table, and called it "King's Sauce Royal." This preparation gives an emphatic answer to the question, "What's in a name?" It is a royal sauce and good enough to tickle the palate of a king.

After having it tested among his immediate acquaintances, he caused some of it to be sold by samples at several points remote from each other. In this way it was introduced into Fort Wayne, Pittsburgh, Chicago, St. Louis and New Orleans. From every point where it was introduced orders came for more, and each successive order was for double the quantity of the one before it.

In July, 1870, Mr. King formed a partnership with C. and J. Conkling, under the firm name of Conkling & King. The new firm at once fitted up a manufactory with suitable apparatus and steam boilers, to prosecute the work on a larger scale. They went into the market and purchased onions, tomatoes and such other materials as are used in preparing the sauce, and employed twelve hands. They kept the manufactory in operation, night and day, from July until November.

When Mr. King commenced he put the Sauce Royal up in half pint and quart bottles only; but the new firm put it up in half pint and pint bottles, and in kegs of five and ten gallons, and in half barrels and barrels. They have been shipping it by the car load to fill orders in New York, San Francisco, and many other points.

Heretofore they have purchased all their vegetables in the market, but they are now preparing to plant five acres of onions and thirty-five acres of tomatoes, and beside this will buy in the market. In order to be sure and exclude all deleterious ingredients, they manufacture their own vinegar from malt and high-wines.

The machinery and apparatus they put up last year was thought, at the time, to be sufficient for the next five years, but they are now increasing it to ten times the capacity. They have twenty men employed on the farm now, and when the time comes for gathering and manufacturing, it will give employment to a much larger number.

This business is in its infancy, but, without doubt, it will grow to much larger proportions. I have been thus particular in describing it because there are hundreds of other industries out of which large and lucrative establishments might be built up; and there is no place where it can be done to better advantage than in Springfield, where water and fuel abound, railroad facilities are so abundant and increasing, and in so rich a farming country from which to draw supplies and find a market for many of the articles manufactured.

ORNAMENTAL CARVING.

WILLIAM HELMLE is an ornamental carver in wood. He does the carving of caps for columns and pilasters, for cornices and all other work in his line of business, for both public and private buildings.

PLANING MILLS, OR DOOR, SASH AND BLIND MANUFACTORIES.

HOPPING & RIDGELY erected a large, well arranged building, during the summer of 1866. and fitted it up with planers and all other machinery pertaining to a first class planing mill, at a total cost, for building and machinery, of $40,000. The work turned out from this factory is equal to that from any similar establishment in the State. They employ from forty to fifty hands, and the monthly pay roll is about $1,500. Their annual sales amount to about $60,000. Near Chicago and St. Louis Railroad.

THOMPSON & NEWMAN put their planing mill in operation in 1866, also. They keep about fifteen hands employed, and their annual sales amount to about $25,000, principally jobbing. Near the old depot of the T., W. & W. Railway.

PLOW MANUFACTURING.

JOHN UHLER has been in Springfield since 1839. Being a blacksmith, he has done general jobbing and manufactured some plows almost every year. Mr. Uhler has not made more than three or four hundred plows annually at any time, and is not now making more than two or three hundred per year.

ROPE AND CORDAGE MANUFACTORIES.

JACOB SCHILLING has been manufacturing rope in this city for over twenty-three years, at his manufactory, in the west part of the city. He makes cordage, rope and sash cord, and manufactures about 30,000 pounds per year. Mr. Schilling uses New Zealand, Sicilian and Missouri hemp, and Manilla imported from Spain, in the manufacture of rope and cordage.

Another small manufactory is carried on near Messrs. Starne & Shutt's coal shaft, northwest of the city.

SICKLE SECTIONS.

JOHN SHAW, is the inventor and manufacturer of a new kind of Sickle Section. These sections are serrated, that is, they are cut similar to an old fashioned sickle, or reap hook. They are warranted to cut equally well in grain or grass.

Farmers who have used them, say they will run four or five times as long without grinding, as those most generally in use. All can appreciate the value of time thus saved.

MR. SHAW will be recognized, by many as the file cutter, who has his shop near Hopping & Ridgely's planing mill, but for the benefit of those at a distance, I would say that his address is John Shaw, P. O. Box 1226, Springfield Ill.

SOAP AND CANDLE FACTORY.

G. A. VANDUYN & Co., erected a factory in 1860, for making soap and candles. The capacity of their soap kettles is 5000 pounds, and the rendering tanks, twenty barrels. In making candles, they use three sets of machines. A steam boiler, twenty feet long, and forty-two inches in diameter, supplies the necessary heat for prosecuting the business. This factory is only a secondary matter. The principal business of Messrs. Vanduyn & Co., is dealing in wool, hides, sheep pelts and tallow.

The factory, is situated one half mile north of the city limits, and the office of Vanduyn & Co. is on Sixth street, opposite the Journal Office.

FREDERICK BAUER is just commencing a new establishment, for the manufacture of soap.

WOOLEN MILLS.

The first woolen mill in Springfield was established by H. M. Armstrong, on the corner of Fourth and Market streets. This establishment did nothing but card wool into rolls, and ran about six months in each year—one poor blind old horse, furnishing the motive power. In order to keep pace with the growth of the city, in the year 1851, the firm of Armstrong & Co.—consisting of H. M. Armstrong, and Joseph and Edward R. Thayer—built the present Springfield woolen mills, on south Fourth street. In 1866, H. S. Dickerman & E. R. Thayer, purchased the interest of Mr. Armstrong, who retired. This establishment was first prepared for carding wool into rolls, and in this way was run for several years.

The manufacture of cloth was commenced about the year 1852. The present well arranged and substantial buildings were all put on the ground since 1860. They cover an area of about ten thousand square feet, and are three full stories, with an attic and basement. They run five sets of cards, and do spinning, weaving, and finishing to correspond, making about 250,000 yards of cloth, mostly flannels, amounting to about $160,000, annually. From sixty-five to seventy operatives find employment in these mills. It is the intention of the proprietors to increase their machinery, so as to more than double the capacity of the mills.

Messrs. Dickerman & Co. are constantly adding new machinery to their mills. Every new and important invention is introduced into their works, and many thousands of dollars are annually expended by them for machinery. They are about introducing a full supply of new looms, which are said to be the finest thing ever invented, and will have them ready for operation about the first of June. During this season they built an iron chamber for the picker, and have erected a first class fire proof coal house. Messrs. Dickerman & Co. are at all times prepared to buy wool, either for their own use or for shipping.

ALEXANDER CORN PLANTER FACTORY.

One of the most extensive manufacturing establishments in this city is just west of the Chicago and Alton railroad depot, and is used by Messrs. Converse & Swannell in manufacturing the Alexander Corn Planter, one of the greatest inventions of the day in agricultural implements. The history of the wonderful and almost unprecedented introduction and sale of these machines, would seem almost a tale of fiction.

The Alexander Corn Planter was invented and patented, in 1865, by T. K. Alexander, of Decatur, since deceased. A re-issue of the patent on the four chamber drop was made, in 1865, to D. R. and John Alexander. The manufacture of the planter was commenced by D. R. Alexander at Decatur, in 1867. In 1868 the patent was purchased by John O. Sloan and B. R. Ross, who removed to Springfield and began manufacturing here—the work being done for them by William Stonebarger. The first year they manufactured forty-two machines. In July, 1869, L. Converse began manufacturing for Sloan & Ross. In September, Mr. Swannell purchased the interest of Mr. Ross, and the firm of Converse & Swannell then began manufacturing for J. O. Sloan. This firm manufactured, in 1870, one thousand machines, which were readily disposed of, and this season they have made and sold over two thousand, which enormous number was not sufficient to supply the demand. The proprietors think it will take *five thousand* to meet the wants next year, and they are fully confident that that number can be increased each year. They have many orders left over and unfilled, having received them too late to fill them, but they will be fully prepared to meet the demand next year. These machines are now sold in nine States, and but a few weeks ago they forwarded a carload to the State of Virginia. They are now introduced and used extensively where two years ago a corn planter was entirely unknown. They are now the best and most favorite machine in use.

Messrs. Converse & Swannell have erected very extensive works on West Jefferson street, for manufacturing these machines, and are almost daily spreading their limits as their business grows and increases. They are determined to keep up with the demands made upon them, and their energy and enterprise, in prosecuting to a successful termination this business, is well worthy the imitation of our citizens and men of capital.

They design erecting at once a three story brick building, forty feet front and one hundred feet deep, which will cost nearly eight thousand dollars. It will be used as an office, sales rooms, and shipping department. The buildings now erected are valued at $15,000, and are arranged with especial reference to the manufacture of the machines. Messrs. Converse & Swannell employ, during the manufacturing season, eighty-seven men, machinists, wood workmen, moulders and blacksmiths. Their average pay roll amounted to $1000 per week. They also used, this season, 210,000 pounds of iron, and nearly 150,000 feet of lumber. Three general agents are constantly employed, besides a whole army of local agents. Their manufacturing season commences August 1st, and continues until April 15th. The sales of the firm, comprised in this year, foot up over $100,000, and will be doubled next season. It has been impossible, heretofore, to supply the demand, but in future they will be found equal to the emergency.

The citizens of Springfield will do well to visit this establishment, and see what is being done in their midst. They will see capital and labor here joined hand in hand, and the practical workings thereof being the financial benefit of the city at large. Mr. Converse has charge of the mechanical department, Mr. Sloan is superintendent of the sales department, and Mr. Wm. P. Grimsley is cashier.

SPRINGFIELD WATCH COMPANY.

This company was organized under the general laws of Illinois, for the government of incorporated companies, Jan. 26, 1870, with a capital stock of one hundred thousand dollars. Hon. John T. Stuart was elected President; Col. John Williams, Vice President; George N. Black, Treasurer, and W. B. Miller, Secretary.

A large room was secured over Messrs. Berryman & Rippon's Machine shop, and stocked with lathes and planers from the works of Pratt, Whitney & Co., Hartford, Conn., together with tools from various other manufacturers.

On the first of May, ten or twelve experienced artisans—who were employed in the first enterprise of making watches in this country by machinery, at Waltham, Mass., and with other companies in the East, and who were the principal operators in the National Watch Factory in this State, from its commencement to the beginning of the present enterprise—commenced making tools here for the manufacture of Watches.

The company secured by the liberality of Henry Converse, Esq., and others, fifteen acres of land as a site for the factory, which is beautifully situated on North Grand Avenue, just outside the city limits, and adjoining the grounds of the Springfield City Water Works Reservoir. The company adopted a design, drawn by the well known architect, J. C. Cochrane, Esq., and immediately proceeded to erect their factory.

At the beginning of December, 1870, the buildings were so far advanced that the machinery was removed into it, from their former shops, and operations continued.

The machinery, which is now almost completed, embraces many of their former inventions and improvements, together with a great number of recent novel ideas. Their late increase of capital stock shows that the company are going to build up a *mammoth establishment, in addition to making watches superior to any others.*

It is but reasonable to expect, with the large experience they have had in building up other establishments, that this object will be attained.

The average number of men employed has been twenty-eight, but at the present time it is thirty-four. This number will be greatly increased, and a large number of females will be employed very soon also, as the work of making the parts of watches has already commenced. It will now be but a few weeks until time pieces from the factory of the Springfield Watch Company will be found in the show cases of all first class jewelers. At the annual meeting of the company, March 1st, 1871, the capital stock was increased to $200,000. At the same time a board of five directors were chosen, consisting of John T. Stuart, John Williams, W. B. Miller, John W. Bunn, and W. D. Richardson. The old board of officers were all re-elected, namely: Hon. John T. Stuart, president; Col. John Williams, vice president; George N. Black, treasurer; and W. B. Miller, secretary.

J. K. Bigelow, Esq., who has held responsible positions, in watch factories, from the commencement of watch manufacturing in this country, has superintended the work from the beginning of this enterprise. Under his supervision, not only the delicate and ingenious machinery for watch making has been manufactured, but the neat, beautiful, and well constructed edifice has been erected also. To describe the building, and machinery, in all its complicated parts, together with the varied processes of of watch making, would require the space of a dozen such articles as this. They will be worthy of an elaborate description hereafter.

GENERAL REVIEW OR CONCLUDING REMARKS.

Springfield has long been noted for its comfortable, handsome and even palatial residences. There is probably a larger proportion of the business men in this city who own the houses in which they transact business, and the residences they occupy, than in any other town of equal size in the west. This has doubtless contributed largely to the stability of its business men. Enormous rents for business houses and dwellings has been the ruin of many a man or firm who would otherwise have been prosperous.

When trade is good, these expenses can be met, but in times of general depression, almost everything else finds its level before rents give way, and when relief comes it is often too late. This very security in Springfield has exerted its influence in causing business to move slowly. If it is dull they can take the world easy, for the discharge of a few clerks or workmen reduces the expenses to a merely nominal figure. A man once established in business, usually remains for life. It will be seen, by running over the business notices, that there is a large proportion of men here who have been continuously in business from thirty to forty years, and many more such could be named.

The fact that business moves steadily and without parade, is no evidence of a lack of enterprise. Springfield has expended more than three-quarters of a million dollars, because of its being the State Capital; beginning with the $50,000 to secure the first location of it here; $350,000 for the Leland Hotel—for which there would have been no demand on any other grounds, and $200,000 for the old Capitol, for a Court House, when they could have built one to suit them better for less money. The interest on the money invested in that building will amount to all of $150,000 from the date of purchase, before the purchasers can have any use of it. $70,000 for the land donated to the State, on which the new State House is being erected, and the city is now under bonds to purchase not to exceed four acres more, to enlarge the new State House grounds, which will cost $100,000 more. Put all those together and it will be found that Springfield has expended nearer one million of dollars than three-quarters, because it is the State Capital.

The people of a city destitute of enterprise, are not likely to expend a million dollars on a single object. The truth is, Springfield has manifested an enterprising spirit, on this question, that would have put her far ahead of any who are now her rivals, if it had been directed to building up manufacturing industries. But it is not too late to do that yet and then have both. The idea has prevailed, for a long time, that a State Capital could not be a commercial or manufacturing town. Indianapolis has has proved the fallacy of that theory. Springfield now has advantages superior to those of Indianapolis; and we believe she will yet give stronger evidence that a town may be a seat of government and rise to a commanding position in commerce and manufactures, and, like the city of Indianapolis, accomplish it without being located upon a navigable river, either.

There are other evidences of an enterprising spirit in Springfield, of which but little has been said. She is the only city in the State, outside of Chicago, that has adopted and carried into effect an extensive system of underground sewerage. This cannot be too highly estimated in its effect upon the health and cleanliness of the city; and yet a stranger may come and go without knowing that it exists, because so little of it can be seen,

Springfield was the first city in the State, outside of Chicago, to build water works. And no other city in the State, with the above exception, has yet done anything that will at all compare with her in that respect.

And I have not done yet. Springfield was the first city in the State, outside of Chicago, to build a street railroad—others have only followed in her wake. And yet she is spoken of as being destitute of enterprise. The truth is, Springfield has been entirely too modest with reference to her own advantages. In place of heralding her enterprises as many others do, she has plodded on in business, trusting to the good judgment of the public in discerning and appreciating her advantages. We believe she will yet be vindicated in this course, but it will do no harm for her citizens to shake off a little of their modesty.

The good influence of this stability in business, is observed in its effect upon society, which is more refined and elevated than is usually found in a town of this kind or any other, except where educational institutions are so grouped together as to mould the public tastes.

In looking over the early history of Springfield, and the account of the public buildings, churches, schools, libraries and benevolent institutions, it will readily be seen that the tendencies have all been to make it attractive as a home.

Down to the close of the great rebellion, it seems never to have entered the minds of the people that any other business could be done here than to buy and sell and exchange the products of the soil, for all kinds of merchandise manufactured at other points. It is not surprising that the situation was thus viewed, because there were little or no facilities for manufacturing. It is true there were two important railroads crossing each other here, but coal was shipped from a distance, and ruled steadily at from twenty-five to thirty-five cents per bushel, and that frequently of an inferior quality. Water could only be obtained from wells, so that a factory requiring any considerable quantity could not be supplied.

Now, however, all is changed! The railroad facilities have been doubled, the splendid water works have been erected, and the immense deposits of coal underlying the city, have been developed at the very doors of the citizens, so that nothing is now wanting but the capitalist with his business talents, and the artizan with his skill—the two to co-operate with each other in using that which nature has so lavishly bestowed and art has thus far developed.

With these resources at command, it may be thought strange that manufactories did not at once spring into existence; but it is no cause for surprise or discouragement that the progress has not been greater. The people here had not been accustomed to think of manufacturing as a source of wealth, and they did not readily, and in fact, do not now fully realize their splendid opportunities.

Another cause of hindrance is found in the fact that from the close of the war to the present time, a shrinkage of values has been steadily progressing in all parts of the United States, and it has, therefore been an unfavorable time for the beginning of new enterprises.

In the face of all these obstacles, Springfield has some energetic men, who have been unceasing in their efforts to inaugurate new business enterprises, requiring capital and labor. In order to act more efficiently in advancing the interests of the city, the

SPRINGFIELD BOARD OF TRADE

Was organized July 13, 1869, with the following well known business men and firms as members:

Melvin & Glidden,
Nolte & Walther,
Ackerman & Nolte,
Ensel & Mayer,
First National Bank,
John Williams & Co.,
Springfi'ld Savi'gs B'nk,
S. Rosenwald,
Smith & Brother,
J. D B. Salter,
Butler, Lane & Co.,
J. Thayer & Co.,
T. S. Little,
G. S. Dana,
J. M. Fitzgerald,
Woods & Henkle,
C. A. Gehrmann,
C. A. Helmle,
Staley & Troxell,
J. Bunn,
Thomas Brady,
W. B. Miller,
Robinson & Bauman,
F. George & Son,
F. Reisch & Son,
J. S. Vredenburgh,
Latham & Co.,
B. F. Fox,
B. F. Haynes & Co.,
Dickerman & Co.,
James Conkling, Jr.,
Schuck & Baker,
J. B. Fosselman,
Van Ness & Ferguson,
Herbert Post,
H. C. Myers & Son,
Wm. Lavely & Son,
Geo. W. Schroyer & Co.,
H. Redlich,
H. E. Mueller,
M. Myers,
J. C. & C. L. Conkling,
C. H. Flower.

S. H. Melvin was elected President, J. S. Vredenburgh, Sr., First Vice President; A. Nolte, Second Vice President.

Directors—A. Mayer, H. Post, W. Lavely, F. Smith, G. N. Black, W. B. Miller, F. W. Tracy, Treasurer; W. R. Cowgill, Secretary.

The following committees were appointed:

On Trade and Commerce—W. Lavely, H. S. Dickerman, S. Rosenwald, Jacob Bunn, B. H. Ferguson, B. F. Fox, Frank Reisch, Jr.

On Arbitration—J. S. Vredenburgh, Sr., John Williams, J. D. B. Salter, C. A. Helmle, E. R. Thayer.

On Railroads—G. N. Black, W. Baker, G. S. Dana, J. C. Henkle, J. W. Lane.

J. S. Vredenburgh ceased to be a vice-president before the close of the first year, and was succeeded by W. B. Miller. With that exception the officers remain unchanged, and the present directors are, Isaac A. Hawley, A. Mayer, C. A. Gehrmann, G. N. Black, W. Lavely, and Herbert Post.

As soon as the organization was effected, the Board fitted up a large and convenient room on South Fifth street, which it occupies at the present time.

The beneficial effects of the Board of Trade has been felt in many ways, but it may be seen in the works of the Springfield Watch Company, which was organized directly through its influence. The establishing and success of the Alexander corn planter factory is largely due to the workings of the Board of Trade also.

January 11, 1870, Mr. W. B. Cowgill, the secretary, made a report to the Board, embodying the result of his investigations with reference to manufactures in the city. He reported $350,000 as the total capital invested in manufacturing enterprises, giving employment to about three hundred men. The corn planter factory was then in its infancy, and the watch company was not organized. With these additions, and the increase of capacity in the woolen mill, and some other improvements, the capital now invested must be near three quarters of a million dollars, and the hands employed about five hundred.

The sewing machines sold at three agencies in this city, for the year 1869, he reported at 1750, amounting to about $145,000.

Of the sale of agricultural implements he had reports from but two agencies, giving sales to the amount of $45,000. From my own observations, and what I believe to be reliable data, I think $150,000 a very moderate estimate of the retail trade in agricultural implements, annually, exclusive of what is manufactured in the city.

It would be well here to enumerate some of the branches of manufacturing that it is thought would be particularly inviting. I have just estimated that the retail trade at this point, of agricultural implements shipped from all parts of the country, is about $150,000—it may be nearer $200,000. If those implements were manufactured here, the trade could be very largely increased, as the railroad facilities are now such as to be remarkably favorable to the wholesale trade.

By referring to the article on the Alexander corn planter, it will be seen that sales for the season just closed amount to 2000 planters. The retail price at the shop is sixty-five dollars, making an aggregate of $120,000 as the amount of sales for the season, if all had been sold at retail. This is but a single implement, of a kind unknown to the farmer, until within a very few years. If factories were established here for making plows, reapers, threshers, etc., the amount of sales in agricultural implements alone could easily be brought up to half a million dollars, annually.

Cotton manufacturing could be done here as cheap as at any other point in the United States. The difference in the cost of labor over the Eastern States would be counterbalanced in savings on the transportation of the raw material, which could be obtained by way of St. Louis, with less than one hundred miles of freight by railroad—the manufactured goods, being in the midst of the best market in the country, would save the freight from the eastern cities also.

There are advantages here superior to any other within the State, for rolling mills, nail factories, car shops, stone founderies, furniture factories, etc., etc.

The immense trade in sewing machines from this place, and its abundant and increasing railroad facilities, with all its other advantages, point to Springfield as a good location for a manufactory of that kind.

The large and increasing trade in pianos, reed organs, and other musical instruments, would indicate this as a suitable place for a manufactory of that kind also.

I might go on, from one branch of manufacturing to another, and point out the advantages for each particular branch; but I will close by inviting, on behalf of the business men of Springfield, manufacturers of all kinds to investigate the subject. You should, in the meantime, bear in mind that the supply of water is unlimited. That if you wish to transact a business requiring a thousand tons of coal, per day, it can be supplied with the present facilities for mining as cheap and of as good quality as can be found anywhere, east or west; and if you want more, the supply can be increased to an unlimited extent.

You should consult the accompanying map, and you will find that the railroad communication is easy and direct with all parts of the country.

In your investigations you could correspond with any citizen of Springfield whose name appears in these pages; but if you mean business, your best way would be to correspond with the Board of Trade, the members and officers of which will take pleasure in supplying you with accurate information on any subject you may wish to investigate. But it would be still better for you to visit Springfield and call on the officers of the Board, who will co-operate with you in finding the best localities for any particular branch of manufacturing, and where lands may be procured on the most advantageous terms. The city council of Springfield is disposed to be liberal also, and will, no doubt be willing to make all reasonable concessions, in the way of water rents and taxes, towards all parties who are desirous of inaugurating any enterprise calculated to develop the industrial resources of the country. The invitation to all is, come and see for yourselves.

THE NATIONAL LINCOLN MONUMENT.

I have intentionally left this article until the last, hoping to be able to announce the day on which the Monument will be dedicated.

It is too indelibly impressed upon the minds of the American people to be readily forgotten, that on the morning of April 15, 1865, the sad news flashed over the wires, that Abraham Lincoln had fallen by the hand of an assassin.

Many days before the funeral cortege arrived in Springfield an organization was effected, for the purpose of collecting funds preparatory to erecting a monument to his memory. His remains were deposited in the receiving vault of Oak Ridge Cemetery, on the 4th of May, and on the 11th the organization took a legal form under the title of THE NATIONAL LINCOLN MONUMENT ASSOCIATION.

A Board of Directors were chosen, who elected Gov. R. J. Oglesby, President; Hon. Jesse K. Dubois, Vice President; Hon. James H. Beveridge, Treasurer; Clinton B. Conkling, Secretary.

Circulars were sent out to all parts of the country, soliciting contributions for the purpose designated. The first act of the Association was to erect a temporary vault in Oak Ridge Cemetery, in which to deposit the remains until the monument could be completed. On the 21st of December, 1865, the body of Mr. Lincoln was removed from the receiving vault of the Oak Ridge Cemetery to that prepared by the Association for its reception, within the grounds of the cemetery.

During the year 1865, contributions came in from all parts of the conntry—East, West, North, and some from the South. They came from all classes of citizens, from almost every denomination of christians, from Jews, from educational, industrial and benevolent organizations of all kinds. The largest proportion came from the colored people, and the children of the Sunday schools.

When sufficient funds had been received to justify it, the Association took measures to commence the erection of the monument. Early in 1868, it advertised a "Notice to Artists," offering a liberal premium for a suitable design for a monument, and invited those interested to send in drawings, naming Sept. 1st as the day for examination. At the time specified thirty-one designs were placed on exhibition. That presented by Larkin G. Mead—a native of Brattleboro, Vermont, but who had spent several years in Florence, Italy—was adopted. The monument to be constructed of granite and the statuary of bronze.

A contract was entered into with Mr. Mead to mould and cast all the statuary, consisting of four groups, representing the Infantry, Cavalry, Artillery and Navy; also, a statue of Mr. Lincoln and the coat of arms of the United States. A price was fixed on each piece and group of statuary, and the Association reserved the privilege of ordering the work to proceed on a single piece at a time, or more, as its finances would justify. Orders were at once given for the artist to mould and cast the statue of Mr. Lincoln and the coat of arms of the United States.

The Association then entered into a contract with W. D. Richardson, of Springfield, to erect the architectural part of the monument. Ground was broken Sept. 9th, 1869, with ceremonials appropriate to the occasion.

When all were assembled at the spot chosen, Hon. Jesse K. Dubois, the Vice President, gave a statement, in detail, of the assets of the Association, which amounted to $158,663 46. Its liabilities were:—Contract with W. D. Richardson for building the architectural part of the monument, $136,550, and with Larkin G. Mead, for the bronze statue of Mr. Lincoln, $13,700, and the coat of arms, $1,500; making a total of $151,750; the payment of which would leave a balance of $6,913 46 in the treasury. The monument would then be complete, except the four groups of statuary.

It was expected that the architectural part would be completed by Jan. 1, 1871, but the delay by the railroads in transporting the granite from Quincy, Mass., made it necessary to defer part of it until the present season. Mr. Richardson now has all the materials on the ground, with a full force of men, and he confidently expects to have it completed by the 4th of July.

The plaster model of the statue of Mr. Lincoln, commenced in 1869, was completed and shipped to Chicopee, Massachusetts, together with the coat of arms, in October, 1870, there to be cast from cannon donated by the United States Congress for that purpose. As a work of art it is regarded by competent critics to be a perfect success.

A newspaper, called *La Riforma*, published in Florence, Italy, in its issue of February 22, 1870, contains a criticism, from a translation of which I make the following quotations:

"The statue, which will rise in colossal proportions from the monument, holds in the left hand a scroll, upon which is written "Emancipation," and in the other the pen with which Lincoln blotted from human history the stain of slavery. As a symbol of union, to which he devoted his existence, the fasces are placed near the statue, upon which is thrown, in relief, the glorious banner of the republic. * * * At the foot of the fasces reclines a crown of laurel—that crown which mankind have unanimously placed on the head of the great citizen.

"But art stops when life is to be infused into inert matter; and then inspiration must be summoned, to express the feeling and sentiment of a soul, which reflects, as in a mirror, the grandeur of the hero whose figure she would model. * * * In this work Mr. Mead has surpassed our expectations.

"The Florentines admire the works of Mr. Mead, and desire to do homage to the memory of Lincoln, who no longer belongs exclusively to America, but to the whole world—an honor to the human race."

Hon. W. M. Springer and lady were in Florence at the time the above criticisms were made, and he alludes to them in one of his letters to the *Journal* of this city:

"The comments of the Florentine papers are very complimentary, and you have a right to conclude that the statue merits all that is said of it. Here, where are found the finest works of Michael Angelo and Canova, and the renowned *chefs d'œuvre* of Greek sculpture, every work of this kind must stand upon its own merits. All who have seen Mr. Mead's statue of Mr. Lincoln admire it."

The coat of arms was completed before the arrival of Mr. and Mrs. Springer. A photograph of it, by L. Powers, a son of Hiram Powers, who has a gallery adjoining the studio of his father, is before me. It was presented by Mr. Mead to Mrs. Springer.

The coat of arms is in bas relief; the shield with part of the stars obscured, supports the American Eagle. The olive branch, having been tendered, until it was spurned by the foe; is cast under foot, and the conflict rages until the chain of slavery is torn asunder, one portion remaining grasped in the talons of the Eagle and the other held aloft in his beak.

Hon. J. C. Conkling, of this city, a long and intimate friend of Mr. Lincoln, was at Chicopee in December last, and his descriptions of the models are similar to those previously given. He says the statue of Mr. Lincoln is about twelve feet high, and that the features are remarkably accurate.

I cannot, in this article, give a detailed description of the monument, but will content myself with a brief sketch of the outlines. The foundation for the obelisk is seventeen feet square, and commences sixteen feet beneath the surface. From the bottom it is built up a solid mass of masonry, thirty-one feet, bringing it fifteen feet above the ground line. To this height it is surrounded by a terrace seventy-four feet square. From the terrace the obelisk rises eighty-five feet making it just one hundred feet above the surface of the ground. The obelisk is twelve feet square at the top of the terrace, and tapers to eight feet square at the apex.

The shaft has a circular opening six feet in diameter from the terrace to the top, where there is a small square room with three windows, twelve inches in diameter, on each side. A circular iron stairway ascends the entire distance. From this room at the top a fine view of Springfield and the surrounding country can be enjoyed.

The terrace being seventy-four feet square, there is a semi-circular projection at the north side, the same height of the terrace, which is called the Catacomb. The Catacomb has six Crypts for the remains of Lincoln and his immediate family. It is entered from the ground by a door on the extreme north.

There is an oval projection at the south side, the same height of the terrace, which is called Memorial Hall. It is designed as a receptacle for articles used by or in any way associated with Mr. Lincoln. It is entered from the ground by a door at the extreme south.

The terrace is reached by four flights of stone steps, one from each corner; two landing over the Catacomb and two over Memorial Hall. The Terrace, Catacomb and Memorial Hall, are all covered with immense slabs of planed lime stone from the quarries near Joliet. This makes a fine promenade on every side of the obelisk. On a level with the Terrace a door enters the obelisk at the south side, and from there the ascent by the circular iron stairway begins.

There is a projection from the side of the obelisk just over the door. The United States coat of arms forms the front of the projection, and this is the pedestal on which the statue of Lincoln is to stand, with his face towards the south.

The entire exterior walls of the terrace, catacomb, memorial hall and obelisk is granite, which will all be in its place early in July.

The Association is not yet prepared to name the exact day for the dedication, because they do not know just how soon the statue and coat of arms will be completed. In order to give ample time for placing them in position, I am authorized to say that the dedication will take place in the latter part of September or early in October. As soon as it can be done without danger of disappointment, the public will be notified of the exact day to be devoted to removing the remains of Mr. Lincoln from the temporary vault to the Crypt designed for it in the Catacomb, and unveiling the statue. The cap stone was elevated to its position Monday morning, May 22d, without any ceremonials except the puffing of the little steam engine that runs the derrick, and the few words of command addressed by the master builder to the workmen.

This does not complete the monument, as there is some work to do on the Catacomb, Memorial Hall, and the outer walls of the Terrace; which can be done more easily after the hoisting machinery is removed from the obelisk.

ANNOUNCEMENT.

With the approval and co-operation of the officers of the National Lincoln Monument Association, I have commenced preparing a

HISTORY AND DESCRIPTION OF THE NATIONAL LINCOLN MONUMENT.

It will embrace a minute historical account of the inception of the enterprise, from whom and from whence came the contributions, with such incidents connected with raising the money as it may be thought will be of general interest.

The description of the monument will be both minute and elaborate. It will be illustrated by eight or ten engravings, which with the written description will give a clear understanding of the whole structure, in all its parts. The illustrations will commence with the ground plan, followed by views of the Catacomb, with its six Crypts, for the reception of the burial caskets of Lincoln and his immediate family, Memorial Hall, parts of the terrace, tablets with the names of the States forming the cordon around the monument above the terrace, ending with a full page engraving of the monument, as it is to be when completed.

Not the least interesting among the illustrations will be a fac simile of a stone —with its Latin inscription and a translation of the same—which was taken from the fragment of a wall built around that ancient city, during the reign of Servius Tullius, the Sixth King of Rome, who ascended the throne in the year 578 before the Christian era. He sprang from the common people, and his entire reign was devoted to their elevation and improvement. For this reason he was assassinated by the minions of tyranny and oppression, in the 44th year of his reign.

After Abraham Lincoln was re-elected president of the United States, some Roman patriots who had evidently traced the similarity between the lives of their ancient king, and the president of the American republic, took this stone from the old wall of Servius Tullius, placed the inscription on it which it now bears, and sent it to Washington City, in order "to associate the names of those two brave assertors of liberty." Before its arrival the parallel had been completed by the assassination of Abraham Lincoln also. By the exertions of the Hon. Shelby M. Cullom, the stone was sent from Washington to Springfield, arriving at the office of Hon. Jesse K. Dubois, September 15th, 1870. It will remain in his office until memorial hall is completed, when it will be removed to that place.

The book will be completed by the fifteenth of August, and in order to bring it within the reach of the most humble, it will be published in two forms, and sent in paper covers by mail, to any address, on receipt of 75 cents, and neatly bound in cloth for $1.00. Address J. C. Power, P. O. Box, 800 Springfield Ill.

Editors noticing this article, stating title and price of the book, with my address, and sending me a copy of the paper containing the same, will receive a bound copy of the book, as soon as it is published.

www.ingramcontent.com/pod-product-compliance
Lightning Source LLC
LaVergne TN
LVHW021429110826
845150LV00007B/2143